HANDS-ON
MATH

Manipulative Math
for Young Children

JANET I. STONE

Photography by Norma Stone and Michele Goldin

Scott, Foresman and Company

Glenview, Illinois   London

To my mother and my father, Nancy and Ted, who showed me how to love children.
And to Laura and Ryan, who gave me a million reasons to do so.

To Gary, who never complained, even about sharing the dinner table with a typewriter for ten months.

Acknowledgments

With very special thanks to:
Norma Stone, for sisterly advice and support and the idea for Activity 108.
Laura Stone, for preliminary drawings and typing.
Ryan Stone, for preliminary drawings.
Barbara Bernstein, for the ideas for Activities 4, 58, and 109.
Roberta Leff, for the idea for Playsheet 21.

Good Year Books

are available for preschool through grade 12 and for every basic curriculum subject plus many enrichment areas. For more Good Year Books, contact your local bookseller or educational dealer. For a complete catalog with information about other Good Year Books, please write:

Good Year Books
Department GYB
1900 East Lake Avenue
Glenview, Illinois 60025

ISBN 0-673-38463-2

CONTENTS

Parts and Wholes 84

Joining and Separating Sets 91

Exploring Tools of Measurement 104

INTRODUCTION

The world of mathematics for young children can and should be a world of inquiry, exploration, and discovery. When early childhood teachers excite young children about mathematics, they can provide more than a good foundation for future mathematical understanding. They can inspire lifelong positive feelings about mathematics.

Hands-On Math is based on these beliefs:

• There is a lot more to early childhood math than counting and recognizing numerals.

• Young children learn best through manipulation of materials and employment of all the senses.

• Concrete activity should precede abstract, pencil-and-paper activity.

• Most early childhood teachers prefer challenging, hands-on math experiences to rote drill and stifling worksheets, but they need a resource to help them provide affordable, easily prepared activities.

• Early childhood education is soundest when it includes parental support and involvement; teachers need ways to communicate with parents about hands-on experience and learning.

How Can This Book Help You?

If you are a teacher of children 3 to 6 years of age, or if you teach remedial math, or if you work with children with special needs, this book has much to offer.

Hands-On Math

1. Provides teachers with math concepts appropriate for children 3 to 6 years of age and with enjoyable, manipulative activities that allow children to discover these concepts.

2. Provides teachers with follow-up ideas that reinforce the concepts presented, result in take-home materials that communicate learning to parents, and provide a transition from the concrete activities in this book to the more abstract activities that will come at later levels. Many follow-ups are in the form of reproducible playsheets.

3. Takes into account time and buget constraints faced by teachers and provides easily prepared activities that require inexpensive (or free) materials, commonly found around the home or classroom.

4. Takes into consideration the needs and abilities of young children, providing activities that are age-appropriate. Motor development, attention span, safety factors, and even nutritional needs have shaped the activities.

5. Combines many areas of the early childhood curriculum with mathematics. Cooking, art, music, large and small motor skills, games, perception, imagination and creativity, language, science, and social skills are included.

6. Provides methods for communicating with parents about hands-on math activities.

How Should This Book Be Used?

This book can be used as *the* math curriculum for the early years or as a resource book to provide basic math understanding in a fun, hands-on way.

Primarily, the activities are designed for children 3 to 6 years of age. When an activity is best suited to a narrower age group, that age group is indicated at the top of the activity. The entire section, "Joining and Separating Sets," is intended for 5s and 6s and is inappropriate for most younger children.

Activities involving numbers and numerals (the symbols that represent numbers) can be tailored to fit particular children's needs. For the most part, 3s would be working with numbers through five, 4s with numbers through ten, and 5s and 6s through ten and beyond.

The main activities in this book, numbered 1 through 121, are concrete; they are designed to precede the follow-ups, which are slightly more abstract. Teachers may choose to use only the concrete activities, omitting the follow-ups. However, follow-ups should *never* be used alone, without engaging in the concrete activities that precede them. This would defeat the purpose of providing hands-on experience before making a transition to a slightly more symbolic activity.

Follow-ups are sometimes in the form of the playsheets found in the back of this book. Playsheets differ from traditional worksheets by allowing for creativity, involving manipulation of materials, and providing a transitional step between strictly concrete and strictly abstract mathematics. Each playsheet may be used as is or modified, according to the needs of a particular class. For example, Playsheet 8 calls for cutting; if your class of 3s finds cutting difficult, do the cutting ahead of time or use a shortened version of the playsheet to require less cutting. Playsheet 3 asks children to glue a reinforcement, a margarine tub lid, a popsicle stick, and a paper clip on top of their tracings; if you cannot collect these items, then, using the idea behind the playsheet, collect and trace more accessible items.

Generally speaking, the activities are best presented in the order in which they appear. The sections on "Shapes" and "Sizes" contain activities that can be interspersed with activities from other sections. The section, "One-to-One Correspondence," must precede "Counting with Understanding," and both of these, along with "Recognizing and Ordering Numerals" and "Parts and Wholes," must precede "Joining and Separating Sets," since learning is cumulative.

The concrete activities may be used with entire classes or at smaller, teacher-directed centers. Smaller groups are especially recommended for remedial groups, special education, and whenever activities call for taking turns. Follow-ups may be completed at centers or individually.

Following the "To Do" section of each main activity, the benefits to be gained from engaging in the activity are listed. Young children are growing in many areas at once, and the activities contribute not only to understanding math concepts, but to many other areas of development as well. Many activities combine music, art, science, social skills, imagination and creativity, perception and language, or motor skills with math, making the activities part of a total early childhood program instead of isolated events. The "To Be Gained" section indicates areas enhanced by the activity, as well as specific skills to be gained from the activity.

The "To Discuss" section provides suggested questions for discussion. Most are open-ended questions for which there are no right or wrong answers. Children's enthusiasm for discussion is directly related to the teacher's acceptance of their ideas. Positive teacher responses such as eye contact, nodding, and comments (i.e., "Interesting idea!") keep children thinking, imagining, suggesting, and participating.

Communicating with Parents

Because parents can play an important role in the full use of this book, much thought has been given to communicating with them about the book's activities. Parents can help supply materials, reinforce concepts by becoming involved with the products and activities children bring home, listen to children who are excited about the classroom activities, and expand on learning through questions and discussions.

For many activities, the book suggests labeling a child's paper in a particular way. Such labels tell the parents the process used by the children and can initiate parent–child discussions regarding the activities. When a paper is labeled "Timed Marble Roll Painting," for example, parents are inspired to ask how a marble was used and how long a time it required. Without the label, discussion about the activity could be limited or it might never occur.

For some activities, it is suggested that parents be asked to send in materials ahead of time. This is helpful to the teacher and lets parents participate in the activities. They become interested in how the materials are used and engage in more positive dialogue with their children concerning mathematical activity.

The directions found on the playsheets, in most cases, are too difficult for the children to read, but they are provided to help teachers give oral directions and inform parents about how each playsheet was approached.

For some activities, Parent Notes are provided in the back of this book. Directions for activities indicate when these should be sent home. Parent Notes provide parents with information concerning math activities and usually suggest ways to expand learning at home.

Needed Materials

Most of the materials needed for the activities in this book are found or collected easily or purchased inexpensively. Many items are already in your classroom or home or even on the playground. Because the activities encourage learning through manipulation of materials, the materials list is extensive, however:

1. The more you encourage parents to help collect items, the more they will become involved with the activities.

2. You may not need all the materials listed because some activities may not be appropriate for your particular class, or you may use the alternative materials suggested in certain activities.

3. Some materials, such as the Big and Small Bag, the Bag of Halves, and the Bag of Parts, can be prepared by one teacher and then circulated among many classrooms, avoiding duplication of efforts.

4. Some materials are used for more than one activity; for example, gift boxes and lids are used for printing rectangles and squares, for matching lids to boxes, for nesting and ordering by size, and for enclosing matching-sized "gifts." If possible, save collected materials that are reusable.

5. Most activities that require food conclude with using the food for snack or lunch. This allows the food to be purchased within the snack and meal budget.

All of the materials you will need to complete the activities in this book follow, with two exceptions: ingredients for recipes that can be found within each "cooking" activity and some items that you will select (suggestions are given within the individual activities) and that will vary from classroom to classroom. You may want to start gathering materials now or, if storage is a problem, prepare for just one or two activities at a time. With each activity's directions is a list of materials needed for that paticular activity.

animal crackers
baby food jars and lids
baby bathtub (water tub)
balance scales and objects to weigh and compare
balloons (red and blue)
beans (lima, or any dry bean)
birdseed, wild
blocks (or colored cubes)
books with numbered pages
bottle caps (smooth-edged, i.e., from shampoo bottles)
bottles of assorted heights, clean and empty (may be plastic, such as shampoo bottles)
brads
broom
bubble-blowing liquid
buttons (assorted)
candles (1 large white one and about 5 birthday or Chanukah candles)
candle holders for the birthday or Chanukah candles
cardboard (found in packaged shirts, or poster board)
cardboard tubes (from toilet-paper rolls)
carbon paper
cards, complete deck
cellophane tape
chalk, colored
Cheerios (or other "loop" cereal)
chocolate syrup
clay
clothespins
coins (pennies, nickels, dimes, quarters, half dollars)
construction paper
cookie cutters (assorted shapes)
corks of increasing size (2 of each) and the bottles they fit

cotton balls
craft sticks (popsicle sticks)
crayons (some in good condition and some old, broken, "skinny" ones for melting)
cups (paper and clear plastic)
cutting blade (to cut Styrofoam)
egg cartons
elastic (one long and wide piece)
eyedroppers
film containers (35-mm, black plastic)
fishing rod and reel with a line and sinker
food coloring
freezer
gift boxes and lids
glue
goggly eyes
gold spray paint
grapes, red and green
greeting cards and envelopes (used)
hats
hula hoops (2)
index cards
Ivory Snow laundry powder
"jewels" (plastic beads, spangles, unstrung old necklaces)
kite string
leaves
lollipop sticks (long) or thin coffee stirrers
lunch bags
magazines
magnet
marbles
margarine tubs and lids
markers
masking tape
measuring cups
mirror
mixing bowl
mixing spoon
muffin tin (cupcake pan)
muffin tin liners (cupcake papers)
needle and thread
newsprint

pail, large
paint (tempera)
paintbrushes
paint-stirring stick
paper clips
paper plates
paper towels
peanut butter
peas in pods
pebbles
pen
pencils
pine cones
pipe cleaners
plastic bags, small
plastic spoons
plastic strawberry containers (with square grid on the bottom)
plates, plastic-coated
pot
pot holder
pretzel sticks
produce trays (from the grocery store)
raisins
records, new
record(s), old and scratched
record player
reinforcements
rhythm instruments
rice
rigatoni
ruler(s)
sand
scissors
shirt with buttons

shoe bag
shoes, old and outgrown
shopping bag(s)
"soft" cans with lids (icing cans, oatmeal boxes, raisin cans, etc.)
spaghetti
spool of thread
stamp pad and rubber stamps
stapler and staples
stopwatch (or watch)
straws, drinking
stuffed animals
Styrofoam, large sheet
Styrofoam packing pieces
sugar (brown)
tape, colored
tape measure, retractable
timer
toothpicks, colored
toy cars and trucks (small)
toy cups and saucers
tracing paper (or thin typing paper)
tweezers or tongs
wallpaper sample books
watches and clocks to examine
waxed paper
Wheat Chex (or any square cereal)
whistle
yarn

How Should You Begin?

With a smile on your face, anticipating fun! The hands-on activities in this book are there to dig into. The brief preparations, slight messes, and clean-ups will be worth it, when you and your children find yourselves looking forward to math. Convey your enjoyment of these experiences; enthusiasm is contagious!

Cross-Curriculum Areas Index

The activities in this book extend beyond mathematics, involving and overlapping many other areas of the early childhood cirriculum. The following index can be used as an aid to planning. It indicates curriculum areas, aside from mathematics, that each activity includes.

ACTIVITY	small motor	large motor	language/perception	art	music	cooking	social skills	science	imagination and creativity
1		X	X	X			X		X
2	X		X						X
3	X		X	X					X
4	X		X	X	X	X		X	X
5	X		X	X				X	X
6	X		X						X
7			X						
8	X		X						
9	X		X	X		X			
10	X	X	X				X		
11	X		X				X		
12		X	X				X		X
13	X		X	X					X
14	X	X	X			X		X	X
15	X		X						
16	X		X	X					X
17	X		X						
18	X		X	X			X		
19	X		X	X					
20	X		X			X		X	
21	X	X	X					X	X
22	X		X						
23	X		X	X		X			X
24	X		X						X
25	X		X						X
26	X		X						X
27	X		X						
28	X		X						
29	X	X	X				X		
30	X	X	X						
31	X		X						
32	X	X	X					X	X
33	X		X			X			X
34	X		X		X				
35	X		X			X			X
36	X		X					X	X
37	X		X						
38	X		X						
39	X		X						
40	X		X						
41	X		X						
42		X		X		X			X
43	X		X						
44	X	X	X						
45	X				X	X			
46	X		X						
47	X		X						
48	X	X			X				
49	X		X						
50	X		X						X
51		X		X		X			
52	X	X	X						
53	X	X	X						
54	X		X	X					X
55	X		X					X	
56	X		X				X		
57	X		X						X
58	X		X	X					
59	X		X				X		
60	X		X			X			
61	X					X		X	
62	X		X					X	X
63	X		X						
64	X		X						
65		X	X				X		
66		X	X						
67	X		X						
68	X	X	X						
69	X		X						
70	X		X						
71	X		X	X				X	X
72	X		X			X		X	
73	X		X	X					X
74	X		X						
75	X		X						
76		X	X				X		
77			X		X		X		X
78	X		X	X	X		X		X
79	X	X	X		X		X		
80	X		X						
81	X		X	X					X
82	X		X						
83			X				X		
84	X		X						
85	X		X						
86		X	X				X		
87	X		X				X	X	
88	X		X			X		X	X
89	X		X						
90	X		X						
91	X		X						
92	X		X						
93	X		X						
94	X		X				X		
95						X	X	X	
96			X						X
97	X		X			X		X	
98	X		X						
99	X		X						
100	X		X						
101	X		X						
102		X	X				X		
103	X		X						
104	X		X			X			
105	X		X						
106	X		X						
107	X		X						
108			X				X		
109		X	X				X		
110	X	X	X					X	
111	X		X			X		X	
112	X		X						X
113	X		X						
114	X		X						
115	X		X			X		X	
116	X		X	X					
117	X		X	X			X		X
118	X		X						
119	X		X				X	X	
120	X		X			X		X	
121	X		X				X	X	

Can you keep your car on the triangle roadway?
(Activity 2, Steer-a-Shape)

Shapes

THE ACTIVITIES IN THIS SECTION provide children with an awareness of shapes, primarily geometric ones. Children explore shapes as they take a "shape walk," transform stick crayons into circular crayons, cut bread and cheese with cookie cutters, create toothpick shapes, stretch a huge elastic circle, and even prepare their own doughnuts! As they explore, they will learn that a triangle has 3 sides, a square has 4 angles, and a circle is a continuous line. They will also discover that printing with boxes often creates rectangular shapes, that recognizing shapes makes it easier to complete puzzles, and many other intriguing concepts!

Activity 1   Shape Walk

Colored chalk
An asphalt or concrete area outdoors
Music to accompany the walk (rhythm instruments, radio, record
player, or tape player)

With chalk, draw very large shapes on the asphalt or concrete that you
would like the children to explore. As the music plays, let them move
along the shapes you have created. Encourage them to gain a feel for
the shapes by moving in many ways along your chalk lines: tiptoeing,
marching, hopping, taking baby steps or giant steps.

Encourage the children to compare the shapes. As they walk, they
may discover that a square has 4 sides, that a triangle has corners or
angles and that a circle does not, that walking a circle may make you
dizzier than walking a triangle, and so on.

Play a follow-directions game with the shapes you have drawn. Tell
everyone, for example, to run to the square, to hide in the triangle, to
sit in the circle.

Let the children use their imaginations to suggest what the shapes
could become. Let the class respond to these suggestions. If a child
imagines that the circle is a pool, let everyone "swim" in it! If a child
imagines that the rectangle is a mattress, let everyone "jump" on it!

Children begin to recognize some shapes.

They see similarities and differences in shapes.

They develop a "feel" for shapes through large motor activity.

Which shape reminds you of something good to eat? Why?

In which shape would you like your house to be? Why?

What can you find in our classroom that is one of these shapes?

From *Hands-On Math*, published by Scott, Foresman and Company, Copyright © 1990 Janet Stone.

Activity 2

Steer-a-Shape

Colored tape
A worktable
Small toy cars and trucks

Using the colored tape, create shapes on the tabletop that you would like the children to explore. Give each child a toy vehicle to push along each shape's outline, using the tape paths as roadways. Be sure to make the shapes as large as possible to provide children with interesting roadways and a feel for circles, triangles, diamonds, squares, and so on, as they steer their vehicles!

Children begin to perceive differences and similarities in shapes and gain eye–hand coordination as they enjoy small motor play.

What would happen if you drove in a real car on a real street that was in the shape of a circle?

Have you ever steered your tricycle or bicycle around your whole block? What shape on the table was it most like?

On which shape would you most like to go for a real ride? Why?

Follow-Up

Tracing Shapes

Playsheet 1

Give each child a copy of Playsheet 1 (at the back of this book). Children may dip cotton swabs in paint and trace over each shape.

Variation: Staple a piece of tracing paper over the play-sheet, and let children trace the shapes with pencils or crayons. They may remove their tracings, attach a new sheet of tracing paper, and trace again!

From *Hands-On Math*, published by Scott, Foresman and Company, Copyright © 1990 Janet Stone.

Activity 3   Box Prints

Many small gift boxes and lids (ask parents to save these for you)
Shallow trays of tempera paint (produce trays from the grocery store work well)
1 sheet of construction paper for each child

Have the children examine the boxes and lids to see what shapes they find. Most will be rectangles and squares. Invite the children to dip the edges of the boxes and lids in the paint and print with them on construction paper. They will discover colorful square and rectangle prints! Label their papers, "Box Prints."

To futher challenge 5s and 6s, divide their blank papers into two columns. Head one column with the word *Squares* and one column with the word *Rectangles*. Draw a square next to the word *Squares* and a rectangle next to the word *Rectangles*. Children print with only square boxes and lids in the Squares column and with only rectangular boxes and lids in the Rectangles column.

Children gain a feel for the four-sidedness of squares and rectangles as they manipulate boxes.

They discover that squares and rectangles can come in many sizes and that they can duplicate them without being able to draw them!

5s and 6s gain sorting skills.

What might have been packaged in these boxes?

What kind of prints would round boxes make?

Activity 4   Dough Shapes

Dough (enough for 12 children)
        Food coloring   3 cups all-purpose flour
        1 cup water   1/4 cup salt
A marker
1 index card for each child
A box of waxed paper
A cookie sheet and an oven (optional)
String (optional)

From *Hands-On Math*, published by Scott, Foresman and Company, Copyright © 1990 Janet Stone.

First, you need to make the dough. The activity is much more fun if you let the children make it.

Mix at least 5 drops of the food coloring into the water. Combine flour and salt with the colored water. Mix and knead. If the dough is sticky, add a little more flour. If it is too dry, add a little more water. This dough may be stored in an air-tight bag and does not need to be refrigerated.

With the marker, draw a shape on each index card. Pass out a clump of dough and a piece of waxed paper to each child. Let the children manipulate the dough on the paper for a while.

Pass out a shape card to each child. Encourage the children to form ropes with their dough and to use them as lines to reproduce the shapes on their cards. First, have the children use the dough to trace the shapes on their cards, placing the dough right over the shape. Next, have the children roll the dough into a ball and again try to create the shape. This time, however, they should create the shape on the waxed paper alongside the card, instead of on top of the card shape.

Give the children time to trade cards and create new shapes. When each child has made a shape he likes, the dough shapes may be baked on a cookie sheet at 350°F for 15 to 20 minutes. When the shapes have cooled, they will be hard enough to put on a string and wear home as a shape pendant. Hardened shapes may also be matched with the shape cards for a matching game.

Children become familiar with shapes and begin to see how they are formed.

They see and feel the difference between an abstract shape and a three-dimensional shape.

They see how heat changes things.

They see positive aspects of sharing.

How did the dough feel before we baked it?

How did it feel after we baked it?

How did your shape change in the oven?

Activity 5   Cookie Crayons

TO USE

Muffin tin (cupcake pan)
Muffin-tin liners (cupcake papers)
Old, broken, skinny crayons, with the paper wrappers removed ("fat" crayons do not melt as well)
Oven
Pot holder

TO DO

Have each child line a muffin-tin compartment with at least two paper liners (so that melting crayons will not seep through).

Let the children sort the broken crayons by color, placing all reds in one compartment, all oranges in another, and so on (or let them experiment with mixing two colors together).

When liners are two-thirds full, place the pan in the oven. Bake the crayons at 350°F for about 10 minutes or until most crayons liquify. *Carefully* remove the pan from the oven and let it cool in a safe place.

Melted crayons harden quickly in the air. When the crayons are completely cool, let each child remove the liners from the cookie crayons. They will discover that heat changed the crayons from straight lines into large circles!

Provide time for the children to be creative with these beautiful circular crayons.

TO BE GAINED

Children see how straight lines differ from circles, how liquids take the shape of their containers, how heat causes change.

They feel the difference between holding and using straight crayons and holding and using circular crayons.

TO DISCUSS

We can't eat our round crayons! Why do you think they are called "cookie crayons"?

Do you prefer using straight or circular crayons? Why?

What other things have you used that melted?

From *Hands-On Math*, published by Scott, Foresman and Company, Copyright © 1990 Janet Stone.

Activity 6 — Stick Shapes (for 4s, 5s, and 6s)

TO USE

Dark poster board, 1 sheet
17 popsicle sticks, plus 6 additional sticks for each child
Glue

TO DO

Cut the poster board into fourths, one for each shape poster. On one fourth, make a square with 4 popsicle sticks and glue. On another fourth, make a triangle with 3 sticks and glue. On another fourth, make a diamond with 4 sticks and glue. On the last fourth, make a rectangle with 6 sticks and glue.

Give each child at least 6 popsicle sticks. Let children make their own designs and shapes for a while.

Hold up the square poster you have made. Let the children observe it and try to make a similar square with some of their sticks on the table. Have the children count to see how many sides their squares have.

Show the triangle poster. Have the children manipulate their sticks to try to duplicate it. Have everyone count the number of sticks in the triangles.

Continue the same procedure with the diamond and the rectangle. Let the children share sticks and work together to make stars, doors, tables, and any other shapes and pictures they want.

TO BE GAINED

Children become familiar with the square, rectangle, diamond, and triangle.

They see that straight lines are needed to create each shape.

Children see some limitations of working with only straight lines and see positive aspects of sharing.

TO DISCUSS

Why did the rectangle need more sticks than the square, when they both have only 4 sides?

Why is it hard to make a heart shape with our sticks?

From *Hands-On Math*, published by Scott, Foresman and Company, Copyright © 1990 Janet Stone.

| Follow-Up | Toothpick Shapes (for 4s, 5s, and 6s) |

Playsheet 2   See Playsheet 2. Provide colored toothpicks and glue.

Activity 7   What Did I Trace?

Many objects with obvious outlines, gathered from around the class-room (scissors, paintbrush, toy plane, record, watering can, etc.)
Large sheet of paper (kraft paper, cut from a roll)
Marker

Before the children arrive, trace the objects collected on the kraft paper with the marker. For each object, trace around a side that best reveals its general shape. For 3s and 4s, place the objects you traced on a table. For 5s and 6s, replace the items (after you trace them) where they are generally found in the classroom.

Ask the children to look closely at the shapes you have traced, and then have each child find one object (on the table for 3s and 4s, in the room for 5s and 6s) that they think you traced. Ask the children to place the object on top of its tracing in the position in which it was traced.

Children gain experience in discriminating among shapes, noting similarities and differences.

They begin to associate abstract symbols with concrete objects and to use logic, memory, and visual perception to match tracings with objects.

Follow-Up   Shape Match

Playsheet 3   Gather enough paper clips, reinforcements, popsicle sticks, and marga-rine tub lids to provide one for each child. Place them in piles in the center of the table. Give each child a copy of Playsheet 3. Provide glue and let each child glue each item to its tracing, in the same position in which it was traced.

If you like, trace additional objects on each paper for 5s and 6s and provide the objects on the table as well.

From *Hands-On Math*, published by Scott, Foresman and Company, Copyright © 1990 Janet Stone.

Activity 8   Cereal Sort

A marker
1 paper towel for each child
1 paper cup for each child
Cheerios, or any cereal that has circular pieces
Wheat Chex, or any cereal that has pieces that are *not* circular

With the marker, draw a line down the center of each paper towel.

Have the children wash their hands.

Give each child a paper towel. Give each child a paper cup filled with both shapes of cereal mixed together.

Ask the children to sort the cereal by shape; circles may be placed on one half of the paper towel and other shapes may be placed on the other half. When all the pieces have been sorted, children eat the shapes!

Children discriminate between shapes and begin to separate sets into subsets.

They feel the different shapes with fingers and tongues as well as see them.

They see sets get smaller as members are eaten!

About how many cereal pieces do you think you ate?

Were there more or less when you were finished eating?

What are some other cereal shapes you have eaten?

Follow-Up   Sorting Shapes

Playsheet 4

See Playsheet 4. Cut many circles, triangles, and squares, all the same color, out of construction paper. Give each child many of the shapes to sort into the columns on Playsheet 4. Provide paste.

From *Hands-On Math*, published by Scott, Foresman and Company, Copyright © 1990 Janet Stone.

Activity 9　Cookie Cutter Shapes

Newspaper
Cookie cutters of various shapes
Clay or dough for each child (see recipe, page 4)

Cover the table with newspaper. Let the children experiment with using cookie cutters to gain an awareness of many shapes. They may cut clay or dough shapes with the cutters.

Variation 1: Use a cookie recipe to make the dough, bake the shapes the children cut, and eat them for a snack.

Variation 2: Let the children use the cutters with cheese slices and bread and eat them for a snack.

Variation 3: Let the children dip the cutters in paint and print with them to create shape pictures.

Variation 4: Cut out the shapes of clay ahead of time, and ask the children to match cutters with clay cutouts.

Children become aware of many shapes and begin to see a relationship between an outline and the area it surrounds.

Follow-Up　Cutters and Cookies

Playsheet 5

See Playsheet 5. Provide scissors and paste.

Activity 10　Shape Hunt

Many shapes, cut from construction paper (5s and 6s can help cut them out)
1 lunch bag for each child
A class of shape hunters!

Before the children arrive, hide the paper shapes around the classroom.

Have the children go on a shape hunt! Children look for and gather in their lunch bags as many shapes as they can find.

From *Hands-On Math*, published by Scott, Foresman and Company, Copyright © 1990 Janet Stone.

After the hunt, have the children dump out their findings on a tabletop in front of them. Let the children hold up each shape as you ask "Who found a square?" "an oval?" and so on. Older children may count to see how many shapes they found.

Let the children take their shapes home in the lunch bags marked "I went on a shape hunt today!"

Children enjoy a game as they practice visual skills.

They see their set of shapes increase as they play.

They improve in ability to identify shapes.

The names of shapes are reinforced as the teacher calls them out.

Look at your pile of found shapes. Did you find many or few?

What shape did you find the most of?

Is there a shape you did not find?

Activity 11   Shape Puzzles

(send home Parent Note 1)
1 front panel from a large cereal box for each child (ask parents to send them in)
1 small plastic bag for each child
Stapler and staples

From each front panel, cut out shapes, leaving the edges of the panel intact. As you cut out a circle, a square, a diamond, an oval, and so on, place the shapes in a plastic bag that has been stapled to the back of the panel. You will be creating a cereal-box puzzle, with puzzle pieces of geometric shapes.

Pass out the puzzles and let the children complete them. Let the children trade puzzles and try one another's. The 6s might enjoy mixing pieces from several puzzles and then completing the puzzles using teamwork. Let each child take a puzzle home, with Parent Note 1.

From *Hands-On Math*, published by Scott, Foresman and Company, Copyright © 1990 Janet Stone.

Children gain experience in completing puzzles, using visual clues.

Familiarity with shapes is reinforced.

Children have fun, see positive aspects of sharing, and engage in a small motor activity.

What were puzzles made of that you have used before?

What other kinds of boxes would be good for making puzzles?

How could your family make its own puzzles at home?

Activity 12   Elastic Shapes

A wide, long piece of elastic (available in fabric stores or at the notions department of discount department stores)

Tie the ends of the elastic together so that it is continuous. Have the children hold onto the elastic and move backward until they form a circle, and the elastic they are holding forms a circle, too! Have everyone move toward the center of the circle and feel and see the elastic circle getting smaller. Now have everyone back up and feel and see the elastic stretch in their hands to form a bigger circle. Have the children move round and round, still holding the elastic, to see the circle move like a wheel.

Let the children take turns jumping into the center of the circle or running around it. Lift the circle high, move it low, let children step over it, and so on. The circle of elastic may be moved behind everyone's knees, backs, ankles, heads.

Three children can make a triangle with the elastic by standing at 3 different points and stretching the elastic to reach, forming 3 angles or corners.

Ask how a square might be formed. How many children will be needed to stretch the elastic to corners? Have four volunteers form a square with the elastic. The 5s and 6s will enjoy trying to form a rectangle, a diamond, and so on.

Have four children form a long, thin rectangle with the elastic by standing at the 4 corners. Have them place the elastic behind their ankles, standing far enough apart to stretch it taut. Other children can

From *Hands-On Math*, published by Scott, Foresman and Company, Copyright © 1990 Janet Stone.

now take turns jumping over the long elastic lines to move inside and outside the rectangle.

Children's familiarity with shapes is strengthened as their bodies become part of the shapes.

The flexibility of the elastic reinforces the concept that lines can be changed to form different shapes and that longer lines make larger shapes.

Positive aspects of cooperation are demonstrated, as everyone helps to make the shapes.

Locational concepts are reinforced (inside, outside, high, low).

Large motor exercise is provided.

Can you think of any other things that stretch?

Stand up. How tall can you stretch?

How far can you stretch your arms, legs, neck?

Get very small, like a ball, then stretch up as high as you can.

Follow-Up

String Shapes

Provide many pieces of yarn of different colors and lengths, with shallow trays of glue. Give each child a paper labeled "String Shapes." Let the children experiment with dipping the yarn in glue and creating shapes with the yarn on their papers.

Activity 13

Spaghetti Shapes (uncooked)

Craft sticks or popsicle sticks (optional)
Glue
1 sheet of paper for each child
Spaghetti, 1 box

Have each child use a craft stick or her finger to spread glue over a large area of her paper. Give each child many sticks of uncooked spaghetti. Encourage the children to break sticks at various lengths and arrange them over the glue to form shapes and designs. Shapes may be outlined with the spaghetti or filled in with pieces of spaghetti moved tightly next to one another to create a surface. When the glue is dry, children may paint over the spaghetti with small brushes, cotton balls, or cotton swabs dipped in paint; this is pretty, and defines the interesting texture and shapes.

Creativity and feelings of success are encouraged because anything a child creates is acceptable.

Children make discoveries about length as they easily break spaghetti pieces shorter and shorter.

Children experience the limitations of having only straight lines to work with.

Activity 14   Spaghetti Shapes (cooked)

A way to cook the spaghetti (it may be cooked ahead of time and refrigerated in a plastic bag until used)
Spaghetti, 1 box
1 sheet of paper for each child (newsprint, manila, or construction paper)

Boil water and cook the spaghetti. Set aside some to eat at snacktime, if you wish. *Do not rinse the spaghetti you will use for this activity.* The starch will make the spaghetti adhere to the paper without any glue! When the spaghetti is cool, give some to each child, along with a piece of paper.

Have the children create designs and shapes with the spaghetti. It moves and bends easily and will stick to the paper, even when it dries out! The cooked spaghetti, unlike the uncooked, curves and easily forms circles, ovals, hearts, and so on. When it dries, it is hard and brittle!

After completing Activities 13 and 14, children can see and feel the differences between hard and soft, as well as straight and curved.

Creativity is encouraged.

The stickiness of the spaghetti, without glue, allows the children to change their minds and reposition it.

The concept of heat, water, and air causing change is reinforced.

From *Hands-On Math*, published by Scott, Foresman and Company, Copyright © 1990 Janet Stone.

How is the cooked spaghetti different from the uncooked spaghetti? What do you think made the change?

What else can you think of that gets softer when it is cooked?

What happened to the spaghetti on your paper when it sat out for a time? What do you think caused the change?

Lie down on the floor, looking like a piece of uncooked spaghetti. Now move as though you are in boiling water. How will your body look when you are a fully cooked piece of spaghetti?

Activity 15　　　　Styro Shapes

Styrofoam packing pieces of assorted shapes (have parents help you save these)
A paper for each child, on which you have drawn 4 boxes (in each box, glue a differently shaped Styrofoam piece)
Glue

Show the children how the Styrofoam pieces vary in shape. Give each child 3 or more pieces of each shape of Styrofoam glued on his paper. Have the children sort the shapes by gluing matching ones in each box. Label the paper, "Sorting Styrofoam Shapes."

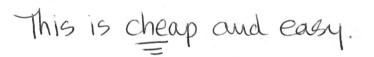

This is cheap and easy.

Children gain experience in visual discrimination and classifying by shape.

What do you think these Styrofoam pieces are used for?

Why are they helpful when we are mailing or moving something?

If we didn't have any Styrofoam, what could we use to protect something fragile when we mail or move it?

Talk about recycling!

Activity 16   Missing Shapes

1 piece of construction paper or manila paper, from which you have cut a shape out of the center, for each child
A pile of shapes you have cut out
1 blank piece of paper for each child
Markers

Pass out the papers with the shapes cut out of their centers, saying nothing about the missing parts. The children will make remarks such as "My paper has a heart in the middle!" or "Look, a diamond hole!" Let the children hold up their papers and look through the holes at each other, seeing each other's spaces shaped like rectangles, stars, squares, and so on. Give each child a blank sheet of paper to place under his first sheet.

Let the children experiment with the markers on the papers with missing parts. The cutout spaces will be of great interest as the children trace around them or make lines radiate out from them. Someone will undoubtedly discover that if she colors inside the shape hole, the bottom paper will soon have the shape drawn on it (the top sheet acts like a template)!

Next, have each child find the cutout piece from his paper in the pile of cutouts you have saved. Children match shape and size (like a puzzle) to find the pieces you cut out of their papers.

Children experience a creative art activity.

They become more aware of shapes and use visual clues to match shapes.

They discover the purpose of a template.

From *Hands-On Math*, published by Scott, Foresman and Company, Copyright © 1990 Janet Stone.

Activity 17   Tracing Objects

A collection of concrete items that have a geometric side to trace (a trash can with a round base, an old record, a triangle rhythm instrument, a shoebox lid, a ruler, a square gameboard, etc.)
Large pieces of paper on which to trace items
Pencils, pens, or markers

Tell the children that you are going to trace around the base of the trash can. Have them guess the shape you will get on your paper. Have the children watch as you trace the base and hold up the resultant circle.

Next, ask a child to guess what shape she will get if she traces around a shoebox lid; let her confirm her answer by tracing the lid and seeing the resultant shape (help 3s and 4s hold objects still as they trace).

Continue to have the children guess what the traced shapes will be and provide turns to trace, and check predictions. When all the children have had a turn, hold up the various tracings and ask the children to identify the shapes on the papers and which item was used to trace each shape.

Children see the relationship between concrete objects and abstract shapes.

They gain experience in predicting and verifying predictions.

They employ logic and small motor skills.

Follow-Up   Templates

Create templates by cutting shapes out of poster board or the thin cardboard found in packaged shirts. Let the children trace with the templates and take home their tracings labeled "Using Templates."

Follow-Up   Shapes on a Fold (4s, 5s, and 6s)

Playsheet 6   See Playsheet 6. Provide scissors.

From *Hands-On Math*, published by Scott, Foresman and Company. Copyright © 1990 Janet Stone.

Activity 18   Circle Imprint

Old, scratched record(s)
Paint
Paintbrushes
Newsprint (larger than the record(s))
A brayer or small paint roller (optional)

Give each child a chance to paint one side of an old record with tempera paint and a paintbrush. Have the child place a piece of newsprint on top of the record and press down all over the paper with his hands. Rolling over the top of the paper with a brayer or dry paint roller adds to the fun. When the paper has been pressed down all over the painted record, have the child lift the paper off to discover the resultant record imprint on his paper! The circular shape, grooves, and hole in the middle will all show! Label the paper, "Guess how I made this Circle!" and let the children see if their parents can guess the process used.

Children see that something old can sometimes be recycled for another use!

They gain a feeling for the roundness of a circle as they paint and press down on the record.

Language is encouraged when their parents guess how they did it!

Activity 19   Strawberry Squares

Plastic strawberry containers (they are usually green and have a grid of squares on the base)
Tempera paint of varied colors, in shallow trays
Paper for each child

Children can quickly make squares by pressing the bottom of a strawberry container in a tray of paint and printing with it on paper. The container is square and the child feels the squareness of the shape as she prints. The bottom of the container is one large square made up of many small squares. It is satisfying to a young child to create many perfect squares at once without needing much small motor skill. Offering a variety of paints results in very interesting artwork. Label the paper, "Strawberry Crate Printing."

From *Hands-On Math*, published by Scott, Foresman and Company, Copyright © 1990 Janet Stone.

Children become more familiar with large and small squares and feel pride as they easily create attractive, colorful square prints.

Activity 20 — Quick Doughnuts

Waxed paper
2 cans of refrigerated biscuit dough
Bottle caps
Oil
A pot
A burner or a stove
Paper towels
Sugar, granulated or powdered
A lunch bag

This is a delicious way to have fun with circles! Give each child a piece of waxed paper to work on, a circle of the biscuit dough, and a bottle cap. Have the children press the bottle cap into a circle of dough to cut out the center. The resultant doughnut shapes (and the circular holes) can be dropped into hot oil in a pot (no more than two at a time). *Use caution with hot oil! Keep children safely away!* Doughnuts quickly turn golden (flip to cook both sides). Cool on paper toweling. Let each child shake a doughnut (and hole) in a bag of sugar to coat. Enjoy!

The circle shape is reinforced through the senses of sight, touch, smell, and taste!

The concept that heat changes things is reinforced.

How did the dough change in the hot oil?

Why is it important to keep away from things that are cooking on a stove?

From *Hands-On Math*, published by Scott, Foresman and Company, Copyright © 1990 Janet Stone.

Attach specially cut straws to make one very long straw!
(Activity 35, Long Straws, Short Straws)

Sizes

THE ACTIVITIES IN THIS SECTION provide children with an awareness of sizes. As children watch big and small bubbles float by, snap spaghetti sticks shorter and shorter, fit cards into envelopes, and compare their present size to their baby photos, they begin to understand big and small, size order, length, height, and even fit.

Activity 21   Big and Small Bubbles

Bubble-blowing liquid
A small bowl
A drinking straw
An empty cardboard tube from a roll of toilet paper
1 pipe cleaner for each child

Pour a small amount of the bubble-blowing liquid into the bowl. Dip one end of the straw into the liquid. Hold up the straw and quickly blow through the other end; very small bubbles will fill the air! Now dip one end of the toilet-paper tube into the liquid. Hold it up and blow through the other end, making sure to press the tube against your face so all your air will be directed into the tube. A very large bubble will emerge! Keep repeating both processes with the straw and the toilet-paper tube. Have the children describe what they observe. Elicit words such as *big, small, tiny, large, bigger,* and *smaller.*

Give each child a pipe cleaner that you have twisted at one end to create a circle. Let the children dip their pipe-cleaner circles into the bubble-blowing liquid to make their own bubbles. Children may blow on the liquid or move their pipe-cleaner "wands" back and forth to push their bubbles out. Compare the sizes of these bubbles with the straw and toilet-paper tube bubbles.

Children begin to discriminate between big and small.

They have an opportunity to compare sizes as they have fun.

Why does the toilet-paper tube make bigger bubbles than the straw?

What kinds of bubbles would we make if we could use a hula hoop to create them? What problems would we have if we tried to make bubbles with a hula hoop? (We would need lots of bubble-blowing liquid, lots of air, a very large container for the liquid, etc.)

Stand up. Who can float like bubbles across the room? How will you look when you pop?

From *Hands-On Math*, published by Scott, Foresman and Company, Copyright © 1990 Janet Stone.

Follow-Up

Big and Small Circles

Let the children make big and small circles by printing with a paper cup and a 35-mm film container (the black plastic kind). Children dip the mouth of the cup and the mouth of the film container in tempera paint. 3s may randomly print big circles (with the cup) and small circles (with the film container) all over their papers. Older children may classify their circles by printing only small circles in one column of their paper and only big circles in the other column.

 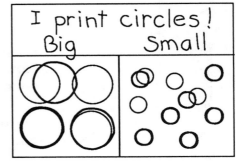

Activity 22

The Big and Small Bag

Many pairs of objects (each object should be similar to its mate except for size, i.e., a man's shoe and a child's shoe, a girl's sock and a doll's sock, a playground ball and a Ping-Pong ball, a large block and a small block, a large paper clip and a small paper clip, a AAA battery and a D battery)
A shopping bag
A marker
Masking tape
1 sign that says *big* and 1 sign that says *small*

Place all of the pairs in the shopping bag; label the bag the "Big and Small Bag." Children take turns finding pairs of similar items in the bag, matching balls together, socks together, and so on. They discover that each pair has a big item and a small item.

Divide a table down the center with a piece of masking tape. Place the *Big* sign on one section of the table and the *Small* sign on the other section. Let the children sort items onto the appropriate section of the table. For children who cannot read, you will need to sort a few items first, to indicate where the big items go and where the small items go. Encourage the children to look at both items in the pair before assign-

From *Hands-On Math*, published by Scott, Foresman and Company, Copyright © 1990 Janet Stone.

ing an item to one section of the table, since size is relative. For example, the D battery would only be big when compared to a AAA battery.

Children see that size is comparative and determine which is the bigger and which is the smaller of 2 objects.

They sort objects by size.

Activity 23

Big and Small Dough Creations

(send home Parent Note 2)
A clump of dough for each child (see recipe, page 4)
Waxed paper
A small plastic bag for each child

Give each child a clump of the dough to use on a piece of waxed paper. Let the children play with the dough for a while.

Next, encourage them to make a set of 2 items, a big item and a small one. To get them started, suggest a big and a small ball, a big and a small pancake, a big and a small fish; then let children get creative!

Each child may show his big and small creations to the class and then take them home in a plastic bag with Parent Note 2.

Children feel bigness and smallness as they create big and small objects.

They realize that a larger quantity of dough is needed to make a bigger creation.

Follow-Up

Draw a Bigger One!

Playsheet 7

See Playsheet 7. Emphasize to the children that their pictures *do not have to look like the drawings on the playsheet*; they merely have to be *bigger*. Some children who are encouraged, even though they protest that they "don't know how to draw a fish," for example, are surprised by the lovely results!

From *Hands-On Math*, published by Scott, Foresman and Company. Copyright © 1990 Janet Stone.

Activity 24

Ordering from Smallest to Biggest

TO USE

3 round balloons

TO DO

Tell the children that you have 3 balloons to blow up. Blow up the first only part of the way and tie it. Tell the children that this is rather small and that you will put more air in the next balloon to make it bigger. Blow the next balloon up until it is obviously larger than the first and tie it. Show that one is bigger and one is smaller. Now tell the children that you will make the third balloon the biggest of all. Inflate the third balloon all the way and then tie it.

Ask the children to show you the smallest balloon, the bigger balloon, and the biggest balloon. Line up the balloons and show how they are ordered from smallest to biggest. Scramble the balloons, and let the children order them from smallest to biggest and vice versa.

For 5s and 6s, you may wish to add more balloons, inflated to various sizes. Children may also order 3 sizes of balls, rubber bands, paper cups, and so on.

TO BE GAINED

Children gain experience in comparing 3 objects, finding the smallest, largest, and middle-sized.

They begin to see that an object may be bigger than one thing, but smaller than something else.

They are exposed to the idea of ordering 3 objects by size.

TO DISCUSS

What size would you order if you could have a small or a big ice cream cone? Why?

What can you think of that is bigger than a man? Smaller than a goldfish?

Why have some of your clothes gotten too small for you?

From *Hands-On Math*, published by Scott, Foresman and Company, Copyright © 1990 Janet Stone.

Follow-Up

Ordering Paper Balloons

Cut balloons out of construction paper that are small, bigger, and biggest. Have 3 sizes for each child. Have the children place them in size order and paste them to a paper labeled, "I order balloons by size!" The 5s and 6s may wish to cut out the paper balloons for you and to order more than just 3.

Activity 25

Boxes and Lids

Many assorted-size gift boxes and their lids (ask parents to save them for you)

Remove the lids from the boxes and scramble the boxes and lids on the floor. Let the children try to put the right lid on each box. Children discover that paying attention to the sizes of the boxes and the lids aids in matching.

Select some boxes that will nest inside each other and scramble them. Let the children try to nest them or line them up in increasing or decreasing size order.

This is cheap and fun. It's math

Children realize that boxes come in many sizes.

They learn that size plays an important part in matching lids to boxes.

Which box would you most like to get a present in? Why?

Can something good come in a very small box?

Name some small things you would like to give or get as a gift.

Get silly — ask them if you could fit in a small box
Bring in large appliance boxes to play in.

Activity 26   Presents and Boxes

Many assorted-size boxes and their lids
One interesting object that is appropriately sized for each box (i.e., a bracelet and a narrow jewelry box, a pair of shoes and a shoebox, a large flat box and a large flat game, a ring and a small ring box, a firefighter's hat and a deep hatbox, a small square box and a small square wallet)

Tell the children that you have many gifts that you would like to put away in the best-fitting boxes. Show each object, one at a time, with all of the empty boxes. Ask the children which box the object best fits in. Let each child choose a box for an item and then check the answer by placing the item in the box, putting on the lid, and checking the fit. Allow the children to reconsider if the fit is not the best possible. Elicit comments such as, "too big," "too small," "too wide," "too short," and so on.

Variation: Have all the objects in the boxes with the lids on. Have the children guess, by observing the sizes of the boxes, what objects are contained in them. Confirm guesses by removing each lid and looking inside!

Children gain experience in predicting based on size and confirming their own predictions.

Through a variety of objects and boxes, they see a number of comparative sizes.

They enjoy a guessing game in which careful observation is an advantage.

If a package is wrapped, can size help you guess what is inside?

What other clues can help you guess what is inside?

Activity 27   Cards and Envelopes

Many greeting cards and their envelopes (invitations, thank-you cards, and note cards are fine; ask parents to save them for you)

From *Hands-On Math*, published by Scott, Foresman and Company, Copyright © 1990 Janet Stone.

Separate cards from their envelopes and scramble them all on a table. Ask the children to match the cards with their envelopes and to place the cards in the envelopes to verify their answers. Stress that there may be many "correct" answers since the matching is by size only. Children who match by trial and error soon discover the importance of considering size.

Children enjoy playing "grown-up" as they place cards in envelopes.

They use awareness of sizes to complete a job and see how knowledge of size is helpful.

They also realize that many cards and envelopes may be of equal size.

Did you ever get a card or letter in the mail? Have you ever sent a card or letter in the mail? Tell about it.

What is the envelope for?

What must go on an envelope if it is to be mailed?

See if you can find stamps and addresses on our envelopes.

Follow-Up

Note Cards and Envelopes

Playsheet 8

See Playsheet 8. Provide scissors and paste.

Activity 28

Graduated Circles (for 5s and 6s)

A set of circular items of varying circumferences (items that have a little depth are best; i.e., pizza pan, round cake pan, round cookie tin, mayonnaise jar lid, jelly jar lid, shampoo bottle top)

Encourage children to handle the items to see what they all have in common; someone will discover that they all are circular. Ask for a volunteer to pile them, one on top of another, with the largest on the bottom and the smallest on top. Let the child try piling the items twice, once with open sides facing down and once with open sides facing up. Next, let another child pile the items with the smallest on the bottom and the largest on top, open sides up and then open sides down.

Results are interesting! Children discover that it is easier to balance a pile with the largest item as the base. They also see that when the items are open sides down the largest item on top covers many of the smaller items and hides them from view. They see, too, that open sides down, starting with the biggest item, results in a taller pile than does open sides up, where some items nest inside others for a shorter pile.

Children gain a feel for increasing and decreasing size.

They make discoveries about how size affects balance.

They gain experience in ordering by size, balancing, and eye–hand coordination.

Follow-Up

Tracing Graduated Circles (for 5s and 6s)

Let the children trace around the items used in Activity 28. If they first trace the largest item, then trace the next-largest item inside the first tracing, then trace the third-largest item inside the second tracing, and so on, the result will be many circles, one inside the other, arranged from largest to smallest.

Activity 29

Block Height

Many blocks of the same size, the larger the better (you need enough blocks to create a stack that is as tall as your tallest child)

Let one child stand up straight while another child stacks blocks until the pile reaches the height of the first child. The first child then moves away and gets a good look at how tall he is, measured in blocks. Let the children reverse roles, so the second child can see her height in blocks. (If children have difficulty balancing the blocks, have the first child stand against a wall while the second child piles blocks against the wall next to him, and vice versa.)

Children get a picture of how tall they are in blocks and are exposed to the idea that we can use units of measure.

Children discover that it takes more blocks to reach a higher height.

They see positive aspects of teamwork.

From *Hands-On Math*, published by Scott, Foresman and Company, Copyright © 1990 Janet Stone.

TO DISCUSS

How many blocks might it take to reach an elephant's height?

Which would require more blocks: to reach the height of your house or the height of your car?

Activity 30

Tape Height (for 4s, 5s, and 6s)

TO USE

Masking tape
Pen
Many blocks of the same size

TO DO

Write each child's name on a separate strip of masking tape. Stick strips to the wall at various heights and locations. To determine where to place them, make piles of blocks along the wall; for example, place one strip at a height of 3 blocks, one at a height of 6 blocks, one at a height of 1 block, one at a height of 10 blocks. Replace the blocks on the block shelf.

When the children arrive, have them look at the strips. See who can tell which strip is the highest, which is the lowest, and so on. Explain that each child must find his or her name on the wall and then build a tower of blocks up to the height of his or her name strip. Have the children predict which name strip will require the most blocks, which the least.

Let each child find his or her name strip and build a block tower until it reaches the strip. Record on each name strip the number of blocks used to reach it. Determine if the predictions were correct.

Let the children point out the tallest and shortest towers. See if any are equal in height; compare the number of blocks used in each.

TO BE GAINED

Children discover that the higher the tape, the more blocks are required to reach it; conversely, lower tapes require fewer blocks.

Children gain experience in predicting, trying out their predictions, balancing and piling, and counting.

From *Hands-On Math*, published by Scott, Foresman and Company, Copyright © 1990 Janet Stone.

Activity 31   Short to Tall Bottles

Many clean, empty bottles of assorted heights (tiny perfume bottles, small bottles that food coloring or extracts come in, middle-sized bottles from salad dressings, and tall bottles such as wine bottles)

Note: If the glass concerns you, use plastic bottles from baby oil, maple syrup, shampoo, ketchup. *Avoid bottles that children should not touch, such as ones that contained medicine and cleaning agents.*

Place all the bottles on a table. Discuss the many types and shapes. Ask if anyone recognizes any of the bottles and can determine their former contents. Have someone find the shortest bottle; stand it at one end of the table. Have someone find the tallest bottle; stand it at the other end of the table. Place all the other bottles on the rug. Let each child stand one bottle somewhere in-between the tallest and shortest, trying to arrange them by increasing height. When all the bottles have been lined up, note how they go higher, higher, higher. See if any have been misplaced, and if so, if anyone can move it to a better spot in the line.

Let each child try to arrange 3 bottles from shortest to tallest. Let 4s and older children try to arrange more bottles by themselves and try to order the bottles in decreasing height order.

Children become aware of increasing and decreasing height order.

Concepts of tallest and shortest are reinforced.

Activity 32   Tall to Short Candles

A clay "birthday cake" to hold the candles
At least 3 to 6 candles
Candle holders
Matches

Show the class the "birthday cake" made of clay. Set each of the candles into the candle holders. For 3s, use 3 candles; for 4s, use 4 candles; for 5s and 6s, use more candles. Light the candles and let the children observe them burning, at a safe distance. Extinguish the candles at different times, so that each candle melts down to a different height (progressively shorter).

From *Hands-On Math*, published by Scott, Foresman and Company, Copyright © 1990 Janet Stone.

The children discover that the candles look like steps; short, shorter, shortest. Remove the candles from the "cake" and let the children put them back in descending height order.

Concepts of height order, tallest, and shortest, are reinforced.

Children become aware that as candles burn, they melt shorter and shorter.

How many candles will go on your next birthday cake?

How old will you be on your next birthday?

Why don't your birthday candles ever melt all the way down?

Stand up. Pretend you are a melting candle. Stop melting when I blow out your flame.

Follow-Up   Melting Candles (4s and older)

Playsheet 9   See Playsheet 9. Provide glue, red glitter, and pencils.

Activity 33   Short Snakes/Long Snakes

1 clump of clay for each child
A line of masking tape on the floor to serve as a straight baseline

Let the children manipulate their clay for a time. Then, ask each child to create a long snake by rolling his clump of clay. Have the children line up their snakes along the baseline on the floor. Have the class help decide which snake is longest, which is shortest, and which ones seem to be of equal length. The snakes may then be rearranged from shortest to longest. Finally, all snakes may be attached to one another to create—to the children's delight—the longest snake of all!

Children gain small motor experience.

They have an opportunity to compare lengths and make decisions regarding length.

They see that cooperative effort can be fun and can produce an interesting result.

Activity 34   Snapping Spaghetti

A few sticks of uncooked spaghetti for each child
1 paper towel for each child

Before cooking spaghetti for snack or lunch, try this activity. Have the children wash their hands. Let each child take a few sticks of spaghetti and snap them into shorter and shorter pieces. Children discover that one long stick can be broken into many short sticks. Have each child hold up the shortest piece she has. Have each child hold up the longest piece he has. Working on a paper towel will keep the spaghetti clean, so that it can be cooked and eaten.

Children see that one long piece may be broken into many shorter pieces.

Children gain experience in comparing lengths.

Children who cannot yet cut gain satisfaction from the ability to make something shorter without having to use scissors.

Can you think of anything that grows long until we cut it shorter and then it grows long again? (hair, toenails, grass)

Activity 35   Long Straws, Short Straws

2 plastic drinking straws for each child
For 5s and 6s, scissors and 1 paper cup for each child

Cut one end of each straw to a point, so that it will fit into the end of another straw. Pass out a straw to each child. Ask the children to try to think of a way to make each straw longer. Give each child a second straw; let the children experiment until someone discovers that one will fit inside the other, matching a pointed end to a rounded end. Let everyone join both straws to make one longer straw. Next, have the children join many straws to make very long straws. Finally, try joining all the straws together to make the longest straw of all!

From *Hands-On Math*, published by Scott, Foresman and Company, Copyright © 1990 Janet Stone.

Let the children pull the straws apart to make shorter straws again. Cut the point off of each straw and throw the points away. Let 5s and 6s use scissors to cut the rounded straws into many shorter pieces. The children love watching the plastic pieces fly as they are cut. Children may collect the pieces they have cut in a paper cup and save them for the follow-up activity. The 3s and 4s enjoy the follow-up, but the teacher will need to cut the straws for the children.

Children see varieties in length as they make straws lengthen and shorten.

When all the straws are connected, the children see the positive results of teamwork and a straw that is very, very long!

Follow-Up

Straw Bracelets

Let the children string bracelets to wear home, using the straw pieces from Activity 35. Provide each child with a pipe cleaner. Children "string" the straw pieces with the pipe cleaner, bend it around their wrists, and twist it closed.

Activity 36

The Long and Short of It!

A piece of elastic, at least 3 feet long
A retractable tape measure
A fishing rod and reel with a line and sinker (no hook!)

Tell the children that elastic does something interesting—it stretches. Show them how a relatively short piece of elastic can be stretched longer. Hold one end; have a child pull the other end and walk backward to make the elastic get longer and longer. Have the child reduce his pull by coming forward again and show the elastic getting shorter again. Let all the children make the elastic longer and shorter.

Next, show the retractable tape measure. Explain that it does not stretch, but it rolls out and back again so that the part we see gets longer or shorter. Let the children take turns pulling it out longer and longer and retracting it shorter and shorter.

Bring out the fishing rod. Show how the reel works to give us a longer or shorter piece of line. Let the children take turns being a "fish," pulling on the line by holding the sinker and walking backward to make the line longer and longer. Let the children take turns fishing, reeling in the line to make it shorter and shorter.

From *Hands-On Math*, published by Scott, Foresman and Company, Copyright © 1990 Janet Stone.

Children enjoy a feeling of power as they are able to control and determine the length of an object.

They see that short and long are relative terms, especially for something that may become longer or shorter.

Children enjoy using adult tools.

Has anyone ever gone fishing? Why does a fisherman need to be able to make the fishing line longer? Why does he need to be able to make the line shorter?

Why do you think elastic needs to stretch longer? How might it be used in the waistband of shorts? Is anyone wearing elastic?

Why does a carpenter need a tape measure that gets very long? If it could not get short again, would he have a hard time putting it in his pocket?

Follow-Up

Long and Short Pieces

Show the children how a ball of yarn, a spool of thread, and kite string unwind to provide longer pieces and wind back up to give shorter pieces of yarn, thread, and string. Let each child unwind a short piece and a long piece of each, cutting pieces off with a pair of scissors. Let 3s glue pieces randomly on a paper labeled "Short and Long Pieces."

For older children, provide two columns on their papers labeled "Short" and "Long"; have the children glue each piece of yarn, thread, and string into the appropriate column; draw a short line at the top of the *Short* column and a long line at the top of the *Long* column to help children "read" the headings.

Activity 37

If the Shoe Fits!

A doll and the doll's shoe,
An adult's shoe
A baby food jar and its lid
The lid to a mayonnaise jar
A child volunteer's hand
A child's glove
An adult's glove
The teacher's head
A hat that fits the teacher
A doll's bonnet

From *Hands-On Math*, published by Scott, Foresman and Company, Copyright © 1990 Janet Stone.

A dollhouse figure
The doll's chair
A classroom chair
A legal-size sheet of paper
A legal-size folder
An 8-1/2 in. x 11 in. folder
An 8 in. x 10 in. photo
An 8 in. x 10 in. picture frame
A 5 in. x 7 in. picture frame

Show the children the doll, the doll's shoe, and an adult's shoe. Explain that one of the shoes fits the doll perfectly and that one is much too big. Let a child predict which shoe will fit perfectly and then check his prediction by trying each shoe on the doll's foot.

Show the baby food jar, its lid, and the mayonnaise jar's lid. Explain that one lid fits the baby food jar perfectly. Let a child predict which lid will fit perfectly and then check her prediction by trying each lid on the jar.

Continue in the same fashion with the other sets of items. In each case, have the children predict which thing will fit correctly and which will be too small or too big. Then, have children try out their predictions.

Children gain experience in making predictions and verifying predictions.

Children see and feel how size affects fit.

They gain experience in visually assessing size.

Follow-Up

Baby Talk

(send home Parent Note 3)

Ask the children to bring in one of their baby pictures and, if available, an item of clothing they wore as a baby. Examine these and discuss how small the children and their clothes were and how big they and their clothing are now. Bring in your baby picture as well, to prove that you were once a small baby, too!

From *Hands-On Math*, published by Scott, Foresman and Company, Copyright © 1990 Janet Stone.

Activity 38   Measuring Cup Order

Waxed paper
A set of measuring cups: 1/4 cup, 1/3 cup, 1/2 cup, 2/3 cup, and 1 cup
A box of brown sugar
A mixing bowl

Place a long sheet of waxed paper on the table. Show the measuring cups and explain that they are used in following recipes. Show the 1/4-cup measure; explain that it is the smallest of the cups. Scoop out a level 1/4 cup of brown sugar (pack it well) and empty it on the waxed paper (it will stay in a small mound).

Next, show the 1/3-cup measure, pointing out that it is a little bigger than the 1/4-cup measure. Let a child scoop out 1/3 cup of the brown sugar (pack it well) and empty it near the 1/4-cup mound. Ask the children to compare the sizes of the two mounds of sugar. Show the 1/2-cup measure, the 2/3-cup measure, and the 1-cup measure in similar fashion, lining up sugar mounds from smallest to largest. Scramble the measuring cups and let the children place them in front of the mounds they produced. Point out the ascending size order of the cups and the sugar mounds.

Mix all the sugar mounds into a bowl and let the children try measuring the sugar with the cups and making various size mounds.

Children gain experience using measuring tools and see the size of a portion each tool measures.

Children are exposed to the names of fractions.

Children exercise matching and ordering skills.

Have you ever seen your parents use cups like these? What were they making?

What could happen if you were supposed to put a 1/4 cup of sugar in a recipe and you put 1 cup in instead? (Show the measuring cups.)

From *Hands-On Math*, published by Scott, Foresman and Company, Copyright © 1990 Janet Stone.

Follow-Up	**Leaf Sizes**

Give each child a lunch bag. Go on a nature walk and have the children collect fallen leaves and put them into their bags.

When you return to the classroom, have the children pour all their leaves out into one big leaf pile on the table. Let the children examine the leaves for differences and similarities in size, color, shape, type.

Give each child leaves of increasing size to order on a sheet of paper. Give 3 leaves (small, medium-sized, and big) to the 3s, 4 leaves to the 4s, 5 leaves to the 5s, and as many leaves as will fit on their papers to the 6s.

Graphing
a way to write → Let the children manipulate their leaves until they are satisfied with their ordering. Let them glue them to their papers. Label the papers "Ordering Leaves by Size."
up the experience.

Activity 39 **Cork Sizes**

Tempera paint
A paintbrush
A paint-stirring stick (free of charge in the paint department of hardware stores)
Many corks of increasing sizes, 2 of each size (found in hardware stores)
Glue
A margarine tub and lid

Ask a child to paint the stirring stick so that its color contrasts with the color of the corks. When the stick is dry, glue one set of the corks, in increasing size order, on the stick (spaced as far apart as possible).

Show a child the cork stick. Provide the margarine tub with the other set of corks enclosed. Ask the child to match each cork in the tub to a cork of the same size on the stick. Have the child place each loose cork in front of the same-size cork on the stick. The child will discover that each cork along the stick is bigger than the ones before it.

Children gain experience in matching by size and become more aware of size order.

From *Hands-On Math*, published by Scott, Foresman and Company, Copyright © 1990 Janet Stone.

Follow-Up   Ordering Corks

Put the cork stick from Activity 39 away and ask a child to order the
loose corks from smallest to biggest on the table. For 3s, provide 3
corks of distinctly different sizes. For 4s, provide 4 corks. For 5s and 6s,
provide all the loose corks.

Activity 40   Cork It!

The set of loose corks from Activity 39
A set of clean, empty bottles (one of the corks should fit into the mouth
of each bottle)

Provide a child with the set of bottles. Provide the set of corks and let
the child experiment. The child discovers that the smallest corks fit the
smallest mouths, the largest corks fit the largest mouths, and so on.

Children see, partly through trial and error and partly through size
awareness, how corks fit into bottles.

They gain an awareness of size and fit as they try out corks that are too
small, too big, or just right.

How do corks feel? What do you think they are for?

Why does a cork have to fit a bottle just right?

Let's fill a bottle with water, put a cork in that is not the right size, turn
the bottle over (over a sink) and see what happens.

Follow-Up   Cork Prints

Let the children dip the loose corks from Activity 39 in paint and print
with them on paper. The 3s may print randomly to discover varied
sizes of prints. Older children may try to print a row in size order.

From *Hands-On Math*, published by Scott, Foresman and Company, Copyright © 1990 Janet Stone.

When the music stops, find a new hat for the hat parade. Choose quickly; there's only one hat for each head!
(Activity 42, Hats on Heads)

One-to-One Correspondence

WHEN WE ASK A CHILD who does not yet understand the concept of one-to-one correspondence to count cookies on a plate, he or she will most likely come up with an incorrect total. Without an understanding of one-to-one correspondence, the child may give one cookie more than one number name (i.e., pointing to one cookie and reciting "1, 2, 3, . . ." before moving on to the next cookie) or may fail to acknowledge the presence of some cookies entirely (i.e., skipping over them or pointing to them without assigning a number name). Even though the child may have learned to recite number names in correct order (rote counting), the total given is incorrect because he or she does not yet realize that *each* item in a set needs to be acknowledged *once* and *only once* and needs to receive one number name and *only one* number name, in order for counting to result in an accurate total. This form of one-to-one correspondence—one acknowledgment and one number name for each member of a set—is basic to counting with understanding.

Children are exposed to the concept of one-to-one correspondence daily. When a child passes out cups at snacktime, the need for one-to-one correspondence comes into play; often, one child is overlooked and temporarily left without a cup, or one child receives two cups and the passer runs out of cups before the job is completed. At the housekeeping corner, a child sets out "breakfast" and matches one cup to each saucer. In the art center, there must be one brush for each child in order for every child to paint at once.

In this section you will find simple and enjoyable one-to-one activities. They lead to the understanding and use of one-to-one correspondence in matching, counting, and comparing sets—skills that are basic to addition and subtraction. The activities provide practice in attending to one item at a time, until all items in a set have been attended to.

Activity 41 — Establishing Oneness

A bag of pretzel sticks
A large bowl

Wash your hands and have the children wash theirs. Open the pretzel bag and hold up one pretzel stick. Tell the children that you have many sticks in the bag, but you are holding up just one. Tell them that when we have something by itself, alone, we call that having "one." As you continue to hold up one pretzel stick, point out that you have only one pretzel in your hand. Tell the children that you would like to share your pretzels and will give each person one. Tell them to have a hand ready to hold one pretzel. Pass out one to each child as you say "one for you . . . one for you . . . one for you. . . ."

Have everyone hold up one pretzel. Have everyone eat one pretzel! Then ask, "Who would like more than one?" Slowly pour the rest of the pretzels into the bowl, so that children see many pretzels pour out of the bag. Explain that since there are a lot more, everyone can have more than one. Give each person a small handful, each time saying "more for you . . . more for you. . . ." With any pretzel sticks that remain, show "one" in one hand and "more than one" in your other hand. Point out again that "one" means something alone, with no others.

Remark that a pretzel stick even looks like the numeral 1, and draw a 1 on the chalkboard.

Children are exposed to the concept of "one versus more than one."

They feel the difference between just one and more than one as they hold each in their hands.

They are introduced to the numeral 1 and enjoy a snack together.

From Hands-On Math, published by Scott, Foresman and Company. Copyright © 1990 Janet Stone.

Follow-Up

Just One

Have on the table many sets of objects. Have a group of books, a group of dolls, a group of blocks, and so on. Have each child come to the table and hold up one book, one doll, one block, and so on. Point out, again, the difference between one and more than one.

Activity 42

Hats on Heads

1 hat for each child, as varied as possible (party hat, sun visor, baseball cap, firefighter's hat, bonnet, sombrero, witch's hat, and so on)
A full-length mirror
A record player and a record, or a tape player and a tape

Show all the hats to the children, making each sound exciting in its own right and perhaps modeling each! Spread the hats out on a table and ask the children to select one hat to wear. Have a hat parade around the room, with a mirror placed so that the children can catch a glimpse of themselves as they pass by.

Play some music as the children parade. When the music stops, have each child place his hat on the table and choose another, donning it before the music starts again. When the music begins, resume the parade, now with each child wearing a new hat.

Children discover, as the parade and hat trading continue, that there is one hat and only one hat for each head. If a child holds two hats, one child will have none. When all the hats are removed from the table, all heads are covered. If there is one hat on the table, there is one head without a hat. If someone does not wish to play, there will be a hat left over. Such discoveries lead to understanding one-to-one correspondence.

Children are exposed to one-to-one correspondence as they enjoy moving to music and making swift changes.

Why is the hat you are wearing special? Does it serve a special purpose? When would you wear a hat like this?

Which hats are good for keeping the sun out of your eyes?

Which hats are part of a uniform?

What other kinds of hats can you think of?

How many hats does a person wear at once? How many socks? Why?

Follow-Up

Playsheet 10

Doughnuts on Dishes

Use Playsheet 10, in the back of this book. Give each child a strip of peel-off (self-sticking) reinforcements; these will be their doughnuts! If snack budget allows, let each child eat one minidoughnut at snack time.

Activity 43

Shoe Bag Game

A shoe bag (purchased at a garage sale or discount store), the kind with 12 pockets for 12 individual shoes
Old or outgrown shoes (sent in by the parents)

Hang the shoe bag up in the classroom and have children place one shoe in each pocket, without skipping any pockets; the job is complete when each pocket has one shoe and one shoe only.

Variation: One block may be placed in each compartment of a sectioned carton (such as one that drinking glasses come in).

Children experience one-to-one correspondence as they attend to each shoe compartment once and only once.

Activity 44

Scrambled Pebbles

An egg carton for each child
12 pebbles for each child

Children place one pebble in each compartment of their carton. Then, they close their cartons and shake them. When they open their cartons again, they see that the pebbles are no longer arranged one to each compartment. Now, some compartments have no pebble and some have more than one. Children again place one pebble in each compartment, being careful not to skip any compartments. When the pebbles have been arranged, one-to-one, they may be shaken and scrambled

From *Hands-On Math*, published by Scott, Foresman and Company. Copyright © 1990 Janet Stone.

again. Repeating the process provides practice in establishing one-to-one correspondence.

Children gain experience in one-to-one matching and acknowledge each member of a set, one at a time.

Pebbles don't really come in egg cartons. What does?

Why does each egg need a special little compartment of its own?

What would your mother and father think if they bought a carton of eggs and then found that one compartment was empty?

Follow-Up

One-to-One Gluing

Still using the egg cartons from Activity 44, have the children place a dot of glue in each egg compartment and then place one pebble in each glue dot. When the glue dries, Activity 44 will not scramble the pebbles; they will stay arranged, one-to-one. Label the cartons "One-to-One Gluing" and send them home.

Variation: For Activity 44, use unpopped popcorn kernels instead of pebbles. For the follow-up, place soil in each egg compartment and let the children plant one kernel in each compartment. The kernels sprout and grow quickly if watered and left on a windowsill. Let the children care for the plants. See if one plant sprouts in each compartment.

Activity 45

One-to-One Popsicles

(send home Parent Note 4)
1 small paper cup for each child
Orange juice
A 2-cup measure with a spout
Tin foil, cut into squares
Scissors
1 popsicle stick for each child (with her name written on one end in pencil)
A freezer

Emphasize one-to-one correspondence as children prepare orange juice popsicles: Have each child sit in *one* chair at the table. Have each child take *one* cup from the pile. Pour some of the juice into the measuring cup. (Use a measuring cup with a spout so each child can pour her own juice more easily.) Have each child almost fill her paper cup.

Then have each child take *one* square of tin foil from a pile and place it over the mouth of the cup, folding the edges down to cover the mouth of the cup. Make *one* small slit in the center of the foil cover with scissors (a slight poke will do). Have each child take the *one* popsicle stick with her name on it and slide it, name-end up, into the slit in the foil, as far as it will go. Have each child place her cup in the freezer.

When the juice is frozen, pass out the popsicles, *one* to each child. Have the children tear their cups away from the popsicles, and hold their popsicles by their sticks. Point out how well this process worked because there was a foil cover for each cup, a stick for each cover, a popsicle for each child. Ask what would happen if someone did not want his popsicle (there would be one left over). Ask what would happen if one child took two popsicles (one child would not have one).

Count the children aloud. Announce the total. Ask how many popsicles there must be (the same number as children). Ask how many sticks there must be. Ask how many foil covers there must be. As popsicles become drippy, ask how many napkins there must be! Have children save their popsicle sticks for the follow-up and take home Parent Note 4.

One-to-one correspondence is reinforced as children enjoy preparing and eating a nutritious snack.

Children observe that freezing changes things.

How has the juice changed (after freezing)?

What changed the juice?

What would happen to the popsicles if we did not eat them and they were left on the table? Why?

Follow-Up   Popsicle Pictures

Have each child draw a popsicle and color it in her favorite flavor's color. Next, have the children glue the popsicle sticks left from their real popsicles (Activity 45) under their drawn popsicles. Each child glues *one* popsicle stick beneath *one* drawn popsicle. One-to-one correspondence teaches an understanding of the number one. Label the paper "One-to-One Correspondence . . . One Stick for One Popsicle."

Activity 46   Matching One-to-One

Wallpaper sample books (ask for free books of discontinued patterns at paint or wallpaper stores)
Scissors

Cut a number of pages from wallpaper sample books; select varied designs, colors, and textures. Cut each page in half. Line up one set of halves across the table. Make a pile of their matching halves and give them to the children. Ask each child to feel and look at the wallpaper design he has received and find a matching design on the table. Each child places his design with its mate.

Children discover that each design has one identical mate and one only.

They gain experience in one-to-one matching, noting similarities and differences, and using visual and tactile clues.

Follow-Up   Patch Match

Cut many wallpaper samples from Activity 46 into small pieces (about 1-inch square). Glue at least four wallpaper pieces down the side of each child's paper. Spread the remaining pieces on a table. Have children examine the pieces glued on their papers, and then look for identical mates for each on the table. Have children glue matching wallpaper designs next to each piece on their papers.

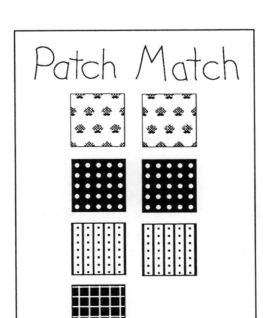

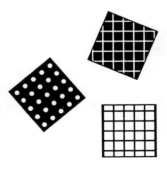

Activity 47   Gift Wrap Match

Used wrapping paper (ask parents to save some)
Scissors

Cut each piece of wrapping paper in two. Place one piece of each color
or design on a table; space the pieces so all can be seen at once. Make a
pile of the remaining pieces. Have children select pieces from the pile
and place them on top of pieces that are exactly alike (one-to-one
matching).

Children gain experience in matching color, design, and texture and in
matching one-to-one.

How can you tell that this paper was from a birthday present?

Which do you think was from a Christmas gift? Which was from a
Chanukah gift?

Can you think of other times that people receive gifts?

What is an anniversary?

What is a baby shower?

Follow-Up   Wrap Match

See the follow-up to Activity 46, but use pieces of wrapping paper
instead of wallpaper pieces.

Activity 48   One-to-One-to-One Buffet!

Numeral signs: 1, 2, 3, 4, 5
Popsicle sticks for slicing bananas and for spreading peanut butter and
jelly
Crackers
Peanut butter
Circular banana slices
Jelly
Raisins

From *Hands-On Math*, published by Scott, Foresman and Company, Copyright © 1990 Janet Stone.

Have the children wash their hands. Explain to the children that they will prepare their own snack, a Cracker Sundae! They will need to follow important steps, one at a time and one time only, to create their snack. If they leave out a step, their sundae will be missing something. Have the children help you set up "stations" and number these with numeral signs, 1–5. Place them in numerical order; if children do not recognize numerals or understand number order yet, they can move to the next closest station each time and be correct.

At station 1, children take a cracker. At station 2, they spread peanut butter on their cracker. At station 3, they add a banana slice (children can peel and slice bananas with popsicle sticks during preparation time). At station 4, they add a small amount of jelly, and at station 5, they top off their sundae with a raisin.

Children enjoy a nutritious snack after using one-to-one correspondence to include each ingredient.

They see the importance of attending to each member of a set (excluding any member makes a different snack).

Children are exposed to numerals and numerical order.

They gain experience in following directions.

Activity 49 One-to-One Stamping

Raisins (left over from Activity 48)
Playsheet 11 (one for each child)
Stamp pads and rubber stamps

Have the children wash their hands, and, from a pile of raisins, place one raisin in each square on Playsheet 11 (no square should be left empty or have more than one raisin). When every square has been filled, the children can reverse the procedure and eat each raisin, one at a time, until every square is empty and contains no raisins (zero or "empty set" may be mentioned here).

Now have each child stamp one time in each square with a rubber stamp. The work is finished when each square has a stamp in it.

Children experience one-to-one correspondence as they match raisins and stamps to squares.

They see reversibility as squares are filled, emptied, and filled again.

They eat a nutritious snack.

They are exposed to the concept of empty set (zero).

Activity 50 — One-to-One Go Togethers

Many pairs of items that go together (e.g., a fork and a spoon, a bat and a ball, a shoe and a shoelace, a jar and a lid, a stamp and an envelope, a Band-Aid and its wrapper, a balloon and a string)

Place one member of each pair on a table. Pass out the other pair members to the children. Have the children match their item with an item on the table. Let each child tell how the two items go together (how they are related).

Children use logic and their past experiences to see relationships and to match items that go together, one-to-one.

What could we do with the bats in the world if there were no balls?

What would happen if there were envelopes but no stamps?

What could we do if there were jars but no lids?

What problems would we have if there were forks but no spoons?

Follow-Up — Go Togethers

Playsheet 12

Collect the following items (one for each child): apple seeds, cancelled postage stamps, pieces of kite string, feathers, buttons, and pieces of ribbon. Have the children match these objects with the items they go with on Playsheet 12.

Activity 51 — Noncompetitive Musical Chairs

1 chair for each child
1 rhythm instrument for each child
A record and record player (or tape and tape player)

Line up chairs as in Musical Chairs, but provide one chair for each child. Have each child sit down, to show that there is one chair and one chair only for each child. Now have the children stand, ready to march around the chairs, and take one of the chairs and move it to another part of the room where the "band section" will be. Have the rhythm instruments, one for each child, piled there. Explain that the children will march to the record and, when the music stops, they will quickly sit in a chair. One person will be left without a chair; this person will become part of the band section and will choose an instrument to play along with the record while sitting in a chair in the band section.

Continue the game until all the chairs and all the children have moved from the marching section to the band section. Point out that, once again, there is one chair for each child; as a result, there is a place for each child to sit down and play music with the record!

The concept of one-to-one correspondence is reinforced.

Children learn to follow the "rules" of a game.

They experience walking and playing an instrument to music.

Children observe sets of children getting smaller and larger.

How can a broom help you count?
(Activity 59, Ring Counter)

Counting with Understanding

THIS SECTION PROVIDES activities that lead to an understanding of counting. Many young children can count by rote (naming the numbers in order, sometimes in rapid succession), but they are unable to use numbers in any practical way. The child who counts classmates to see how many birthday party invitations he or she needs to buy uses numbers with understanding.

As children count "quills" on their porcupines, count peanut butter balls they have created and will eat, make a noodle necklace of a particular number, see how many children will fit inside a hula hoop, and hang sets of clothespins on the playground fence, they engage in two types of counting activities: creating sets of a given number, and finding out the number of items in a given set.

This section also exposes children to the concepts of more, fewer, and equal and provides experience with estimating.

From *Hands-On Math*, published by Scott, Foresman and Company, Copyright © 1990 Janet Stone.

Activity 52

Table of 1

A large numeral 1 to hold up and later place on the table
A table
1 paper plate for each child
A name strip for each child
Objects commonly found around the classroom

Hold up the numeral 1, written on a large paper. Next, tell the children that this is called *one*. Let the children "write" a 1 in the air with their arm, finger extended. Repeat this many times, encouraging the children to make their 1 from top to bottom and to say the word *one* as they "write." Explain that the 1 stands for something all alone, for a set of a thing by itself; show 1 book, 1 pencil, 1 block, and so on. Place the large numeral 1 in the center of the table. Line paper plates around the edges of the table, with a name strip above each plate. Explain that this will be the "Table of 1."

Each child will need to find *one* object in the room to place on the Table of 1; each child will place his set of 1 on the paper plate below his name strip. Let the children walk about the room and decide on their one item. When each child has completed the set on his plate, have everyone notice all the sets of 1 on the Table of 1. If any plate has more than 1 item, encourage the set maker to put back items until the set has just 1 thing. Point to each plate, announce the set maker's name and have that child count the items in the set; of course, all will equal 1.

Children begin to identify the numeral 1, and to understand the concept of a set of 1.

They create their own set of 1.

Follow-Up

Set of 1

Write the numeral 1 on each child's sheet of paper. Each child selects one item from a pile of things to glue on her paper, to create a set of 1. Items to glue might include fallen leaves, drinking straws, popsicle sticks, small rocks, jar lids, plastic coffee scoops, etc. Label the papers "I make a set of 1."

Activity 53   Table of 2

A large numeral 1
Objects commonly found around the classroom
A large numeral 2
A table
A paper plate for each child
A name strip for each child

Hold up the numeral 1 and remind the children of the Table of 1 created in Activity 52. Show some of the items that were on the Table of 1, such as 1 crayon, 1 ball, and so on. Now tell the children that if we add another item to a set of just 1 item, we will have more—we will have a set of 2. Ask a child to get another crayon and place it next to the 1 crayon we had.

Now show the set of 2 crayons. Hold 1 crayon in each hand and hold them up as you count, "One, two. We now have two crayons." Ask someone to make a set of 2 balls, adding to the set of 1 ball. Count the balls together. "One, two. We have two balls." Show the children how, when we have 2, there is 1 for each of our hands. Show the numeral 2 and explain that this is called *two*. Place the numeral on the table and suggest that today the class create a Table of 2.

Line up paper plates along the edges of the table, each under a child's name strip. Ask the children to walk about the room and find a set of 2 objects to place on their plates. When all sets are complete, have the children notice all the sets of 2. Point out that sets of 2 may have matching objects or objects that do not match. Have each child count his set aloud and tell how many objects there are.

Note: Each number you teach may be introduced in a similar manner. Have a Table of 3, a Table of 4, and so on. Of course, many experiences involving a number should be presented before a new number is introduced.

Children are introduced to the numeral 2 and to the number of items it represents.

Children compare 1 to 2 and create their own set of 2.

From *Hands-On Math*, published by Scott, Foresman and Company, Copyright © 1990 Janet Stone.

Follow-Up

Two Feet

Have each child stand on a piece of paper while you trace around her feet or shoes with a crayon. Have the child count the foot tracings. Label the paper, "I have two feet!" (5s and 6s may find partners and trace around one another's shoes.)

Activity 54

Twoness

A stapler and staples
Carbon paper for each child
2 pieces of newsprint or typing paper for each child
A pencil or pen for each child

For each child, staple a piece of carbon paper, shiny side down, between two pieces of typing paper or newsprint. Invite the children to draw on the top paper. When drawings are complete, ask the children to pull the papers apart. They discover that they have created two drawings at once! Let them experiment further with carbon paper, creating more duplicates.

The concept of twoness is reinforced as children enjoy creative art and discover the purpose of carbon paper.

How is carbon paper used in an office?

Would it work if you turned the shiny side up? Let's find out!

How many pictures would you get if you used three pieces of paper with two sheets of carbon paper in-between?

Activity 55

Pairs of Gloves

Books of wallpaper samples (wallpaper stores will give you books of discontinued styles, free of charge)
Crayons
Scissors

From *Hands-On Math*, published by Scott, Foresman and Company, Copyright © 1990 Janet Stone.

Trace each child's hands on wallpaper samples, using a different design for each child (5s and 6s may be able to trace partner's hands). Cut tracings out (5s and 6s may be able to cut out outlines of their own hands). Mix all the wallpaper gloves on the table. Let children find matching gloves and place them in pairs.

Children discover that pairs are sets of 2.

They observe differences in their left and right hands.

They match wallpaper designs.

If they trace and cut, they gain small motor experience.

Follow-Up	Mitten Match
Playsheet 13	Provide each child with scissors, glue, and Playsheet 13.

Activity 56 Pairs of Shoes

Shoes that the children are wearing
Pairs of shoes collected for Activity 43

Have all the children remove their shoes. Scramble them in a pile. For 5s and 6s, add shoes collected for Activity 43 to increase the challenge. Let the children take turns placing the shoes in matching pairs (sets of 2). Have children find their own shoes again and put them on, pointing out that each person needs 2 shoes.

The concept of twoness is reinforced.

Children see likenesses and differences as they find matching pairs of shoes.

Children gain small motor experience, and an experience in independence, as they try to put their own shoes back on.

The idea of pairs as sets of 2 is reinforced.

From *Hands-On Math*, published by Scott, Foresman and Company, Copyright © 1990 Janet Stone.

Activity 57 — Pairs Bag

TO USE

Items that are used in pairs (a pair of shoes, a pair of socks, a pair of earrings, a pair of dice, a pair of mittens, a pair of cymbals, a pair of identical salt and pepper shakers)
A shopping bag

TO DO

Place all the pairs in the shopping bag. Have the children remove the articles from the shopping bag and place them in matching pairs. Then, let the children return the articles to the bag so others can play with it.

TO BE GAINED

The concept of pairs as sets of 2 is reinforced.

Children use visual discrimination to find matching pairs.

TO DISCUSS

Can you think of other things that come in pairs?

What is the pair of dice used for? Can anyone count the dots on a side of one die?

A pair of pants is really only one object. Why is it called a "pair"?

Activity 58 — Making Snowmen

TO USE

A 1/4-cup measure
Ivory Snow laundry powder, in a large bowl
A paper cup for each child
A measuring tablespoon
Water, in a small bowl
1 small, white paper plate for each child
Uncooked spaghetti
2 raisins for each child
Small top hats made from black construction paper
Glue

TO DO

Have each child use the 1/4-cup measure to place 1/4-cup of Ivory Snow in her paper cup. Have each child use the tablespoon to add 1 tablespoon of water to her cup. Have the children use their hands to stir and squeeze the mixture until a pliable glob of "snow" has been formed. The glob can then be placed on the paper plate.

Have the children pull the glob apart and roll out 3 balls. Children then build snowmen with their balls of "snow." These will stick to each other, and the bottom ball will stick to the plate. When all 3 balls are attached, one on top of the other, children add arms, using pieces of uncooked spaghetti.

The 2 arms will stick easily into the middle snowball. Children may add 2 raisin eyes by poking short pieces of uncooked spaghetti through the raisins and into the snowman's head. A little piece of spaghetti may be glued to the top hat, and this will easily stick into the top of the snowman. For older children, other accessories (broom, mittens) may be cut out and glued to the spaghetti arms.

Have the children count again to review the number of eyes, hats, arms, snowballs, and snowmen!

Children review counting through 3.

A set of 3 is reinforced as children roll out and use 3 "snowballs."

The activity smells, feels, and looks good, making use of 3 of the senses!

How is this snow different from real snow?

How is it like real snow?

Why do your hands look so clean after this project?

Activity 59   Ring Counter

Index cards with large numerals written on them
A broom
Any set of rings, larger than a broom handle (shower curtain rings, rings that hold a six-pack of soda cans together, plastic bracelets, or toilet-paper rolls that have been cut apart into rings and decorated with markers by the class)

Pass out number cards so that each child has one. Have two children hold a broom up so that it is parallel to the floor. Let each child have a turn placing a number card in the broom's bristles (holding the card for all to see) and placing rings on the handle to create a set of the number the card indicates. As the child adds each ring to the handle, the class can help him count aloud until the desired number is reached. The child removes his number card and rings so the next child can use the ring counter.

From *Hands-On Math*, published by Scott, Foresman and Company, Copyright © 1990 Janet Stone.

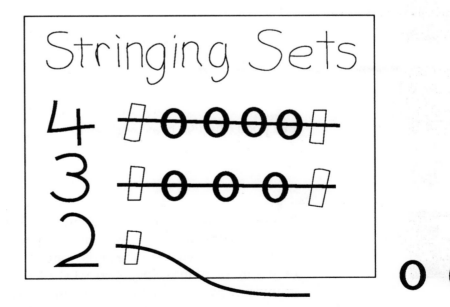

TO BE GAINED

Children enjoy using this simple "machine."

Numerals and numbers are reinforced, eye–hand coordination is employed, and cooperative activity is encouraged.

The ring counter allows for easy correcting of counting mistakes, as rings are easily added or subtracted.

Follow-Up

Stringing Sets

Using tape, attach 4 colored strings or pieces of yarn by one end to a sheet of paper. Near each string, write a numeral that the children recognize. Provide Cheerios or other loop-shaped cereal for the children to count and string. When a string has the appropriate number of Cheerios, have the child secure the loose end of the string to the paper with a piece of tape. Label the paper, "Stringing Sets."

Activity 60   Counting Peanut Butter Balls

Peanut butter balls (enough for 12 children)
     1 cup peanut butter
     1 cup corn syrup
     1-1/4 cup nonfat dry milk
     1-1/4 cup confectioner's sugar
A bowl
A large spoon
Waxed paper

Have the children wash their hands.

Let the children help measure and mix all the ingredients for peanut butter Playdough in the bowl.

Give each child a clump of the peanut butter Playdough on a sheet of waxed paper. Have each child roll 1 peanut butter ball. Next, have each child create 2 balls. Continue until each child has created 5 balls. Let the children eat some of the peanut butter balls, then have each child tell how many balls are left. Let the children eat the rest. When all are eaten, ask how many are left now; briefly discuss zero (also called the empty set).

Children enjoy a cooking activity, and small motor activity, as counting through 5 is reinforced.

Children see their sets increase in number and then decrease to zero.

Activity 61   Peas in Pods

Pea pods (English peas work well)
A paper cup for each child

Before cooking peas for snack or lunch, have children wash their hands. Give each child at least one pea pod, and a paper cup to hold the peas. Children open the pods, remove the peas, and count them as they drop them into a paper cup. Let each child announce the total number of peas she finds. See who finds the most. Peas may be eaten raw, or cooked in boiling water (or both, for comparison). Also try finding and counting seeds in apples, oranges, tangerines, pole beans, and so on. Seeds may be planted.

From *Hands-On Math*, published by Scott, Foresman and Company, Copyright © 1990 Janet Stone.

Children enjoy counting natural objects, right from their natural container!

Counting and small motor skills are reinforced as the peas are shelled.

Children associate positive feelings with counting as they complete this adultlike task.

Activity 62

Fill Your Plate

1 plastic-coated, disposable plate for each child
Crayons
Paper towels
Cutout pictures of foods from magazines and newspapers

You can find plastic-coated, disposable party plates in dime stores or party goods stores that can be written on with crayons and then erased with paper towels. Write one child's name on each plate with a crayon. Under the name, write a numeral that the child recognizes. Place cutout pictures of foods on the table with the plates. Let the children put as many food cutouts on their plates as their numeral indicates. As the children learn to recognize higher numerals, erase numerals you have written and write new ones on the plates, letting the children form sets of higher numbers. Children can also create sets of pencils, crayons, beads, paper clips, and so on, on their plates, if food pictures are not handy.

Recognition of numerals and the child's name is reinforced.

Children gain experience making choices and counting members of sets.

Opportunity is presented for discussing healthy foods.

What are some of the foods you like that we did not have pictures of?

Who can name some foods that have empty calories, that do not help us grow and stay healthy?

Who can name some foods that help us grow and stay healthy?

Did you choose some of these for your plate?

From *Hands-On Math*, published by Scott, Foresman and Company, Copyright © 1990 Janet Stone.

Activity 63 — Use-Your-Noodle Necklaces

TO USE

Uncooked rigatoni
Paper cups
Water
Food coloring (assorted colors)
Plastic spoons
Paper towels (placed over newspaper, to protect tabletop)
Lacing, yarn or string
Small tags for each necklace that say, "I counted to ___"

TO DO

Let the children dye the rigatoni: Fill paper cups about one-third of the way with water. Add food coloring until the color is bright. Have the children drop a few rigatoni noodles into the colored water and stir gently with plastic spoons. When the rigatoni has enough color, have the children spoon the rigatoni onto the paper towels, and dye a few more pieces. Let the rigatoni dry overnight. Be sure to space pieces so they do not stick to one another. They will look like brightly colored beads.

Assign each child a number of rigatoni noodles to count out and string. Attach a tag and fill in the number of rigatoni the child counted. (*Hint:* To keep the rigatoni from falling off as the child is stringing, tie a loose knot around the first piece strung. Untie the knot when the stringing is completed and tie the necklace closed.)

TO BE GAINED

This activity allows for individualization, as you can give each child a number to count up to that he has mastered.

Color perception, small motor skill, counting with understanding, and numeral recognition are reinforced.

Activity 64 — Action Sets

TO USE

As you expose children to higher counting, let the children create interesting sets through actions. Children especially enjoy using adultlike tools to create sets. For example:

TO DO

Children punch holes with a hole puncher the number of times a numeral indicates

Children use a stapler to create sets of particular numbers of staples (supervise)

From *Hands-On Math*, published by Scott, Foresman and Company, Copyright © 1990 Janet Stone.

TO DISCUSS

If we put small babies in the hoop, could we fit more people? Why?

What else can you do with a hula hoop? Who will show us?

Follow-Up	Stick Fit
Playsheet 14	Provide each child with glue, popsicle sticks, and Playsheet 14.

Activity 66 — Mind Reading (for 5s and 6s)

TO USE

Children who want to read each other's minds!

TO DO

Tell the children to think of a number they have learned, but not to tell anyone the number. Call on a volunteer to stand before the class and think about his number. Then have him select an action (blinking, hopping, sneezing, quacking, hiccuping, etc.) and complete it as many times as the number chosen dictates. Children "read his mind" by counting softly to themselves until his actions are complete. They raise their hands when they know the total.

TO BE GAINED

Children gain experience in counting actions instead of objects and in keeping mental track of numbers.

TO DISCUSS

How did counting help you "mind read"?

Were you really reading his or her mind?

Activity 67 — Create It Equal!

TO USE

Masking tape or colored tape
Blocks or colored cubes to count

From *Hands-On Math*, published by Scott, Foresman and Company, Copyright © 1990 Janet Stone.

On a tabletop, create two large squares with tape. In the first square, create a set of 4 blocks. Ask for a volunteer to create another set of 4 blocks inside the second square. Point out that the two sets are *equal*; they have the same number of members.

Build a set of 6 blocks in the first square. Let a child make a set *equal* to this in the second square. Remind her that equal means having the same number.

Continue creating sets in the first square and letting the children create equal sets in the second square, until everyone has had a turn. Try using different numbers of items and different items, such as pencils, chalk, paintbrushes, plastic animals, and so on.

Children are introduced to the concept of equal.

Children create sets that are equal to others.

Activity 68   Make an Equal Set

5 volunteers
5 chairs
2 margarine tubs
3 margarine tub lids
3 toy saucers
3 toy tea cups
An old button-down shirt, with all its buttons
Scissors
Needle and thread
1 paper cup and 1 drinking straw for each child

Ask 5 children to stand in front of the class. Count them aloud and state, "We have five children standing. If they want to sit down, we will need an *equal* set of chairs; we will need five chairs." Ask a child in the class to line up 5 chairs in front of the class, and to count them aloud. Ask the 5 children to sit in the 5 chairs and state, "Five children *equal* five chairs."

Now ask, "What would happen if we only had four chairs?" Ask the 5 seated children to stand and remove 1 chair. Count the children aloud again, stating that there is a set of 5 children. Count the chairs again, stating that there is a set of 4 chairs. Explain that the sets of children and chairs are no longer equal; they are *unequal*. Have the children sit down again; 1 child will have to remain standing. Explain that this is because there are *more* children than chairs. Have the children return to their class seats.

Show the margarine tubs. Have a child count them to show there is a set of 2. Take out the 3 margarine tub lids. Ask for a volunteer to make a set of lids that is *equal* to the set of tubs, pointing out that this means we need a set of lids that has as many as the set of tubs. Verify the response by having the child match the set of lids to the set of tubs; if each tub has a lid and there are no leftover lids, the sets are equal. Show that if we try to use the third lid, the sets become unequal; there are *more* lids than tubs.

Show the set of saucers. Have a volunteer count them. State that there are 3 saucers. Ask how many cups we need to make an equal set. Show the set of 3 saucers and 3 cups. Ask if the sets are equal. Take away a cup. Ask if they are equal now. Have a child place a cup on each saucer; show how sets match, one-to-one, when they are equal.

Show the button-down shirt. Have a volunteer count the buttons aloud. Ask how many *buttonholes* there must be. State that in order for the shirt to stay completely closed, the number of buttons must equal the number of buttonholes in a shirt. Ask a volunteer to button all the buttons. Point out that there is a hole for each button. Point out that the set of buttons equals the set of buttonholes. Ask what happens when we lose a button (i.e., the shirt does not stay closed as it should, there are more holes than buttons, there is a hole with no button, we need to sew on a button). Cut a button off and show how the set of buttons and the set of holes are now unequal. Sew the button back on to make the sets equal again.

Have a volunteer count the number of children in the class (for example, 12). Ask a child to make an equal set of cups on the table, so that each child will have 1 cup for juice time. When the set of 12 cups has been created, have the child pass out the cups to see that the set of children equals the set of cups. Follow the same procedure with drinking straws, having a child create a set of straws equal to the set of children and then match each straw to a child. Enjoy juice time!

TO BE GAINED

Children are introduced to the concepts of equal, unequal, and more.

Children see and experience the changing of sets as they increase and decrease in number.

Their knowledge of one-to-one correspondence is reinforced and put into practice as sets are made equal to others.

From *Hands-On Math*, published by Scott, Foresman and Company, Copyright © 1990 Janet Stone.

Follow-Up

Playsheet 15

Bean Sets

Provide children with beans and Playsheet 15 and glue or soil (optional).

Activity 69

More or Fewer

2 hula hoops (or circles made of tape or yarn)
Sets of objects to fit in the hoops (i.e., feathers, buttons, paintbrushes, popsicle sticks, straws)

In one hoop, place a set of 1 feather. In the other hoop, ask a child to make another set of feathers, making sure that the second set has *more* feathers than the first. When he has made his set, point out the set that has more and the set that has fewer. Count each set aloud to verify your labels. ("Yes, a set of 1 has fewer feathers than a set of 5. A set of 5 has more feathers than a set of 1.")

Next, make a set of 2 buttons in one hoop and ask a child to make a set of more buttons in the other hoop. When she has made her set, point out the set that has fewer and the set that has more. Again, count aloud to verify the "fewer" and "more" labels.

Make a set of 6 crayons in one hoop. Ask a child to make a set of fewer crayons—less than 6—in the other hoop. When he finishes, compare the sets by counting each one. Have the class help you decide which set has fewer members and which set has more. Continue making and comparing sets until everyone has had a turn. If a set has more members than a child can count, show how a member from one set can be matched with a member of the other set until all the members of one set are used up; the other set will be the set with more. Let children try this matching, one-to-one, to compare sets, discovering which has more and which has fewer.

The concepts of *more* and *fewer* are presented.

Children create sets of more and fewer members.

One-to-one correspondence is reinforced as it is used to compare set sizes.

| Follow-Up | The More, the Merrier! |

Playsheet 16 Provide each child with crayons and Playsheet 16.

Activity 70 Guess, Then Count!

Sets of items on a table (a set of pennies, a set of spools of thread, a set of balls of clay, a set of paper cups, a set of marbles)
Numeral signs that identify the number of members in the sets shown

Show the set of cups, for example. Tell the children to guess how many cups there are, without giving time for them to actually count. Record their answers on the chalkboard. Now, count the cups slowly and clearly. See if any of the guesses were correct. See which guesses were close to being correct. Point out that we can guess or estimate a number, but that counting lets us be exact. Place the appropriate numeral card in front of the set of cups.

Next, show the set of pennies, for example. Again, let the children guess the number of pennies in the set. Have a child count the pennies and place the appropriate numeral sign in front of the set.

Continue to number the sets, first with guesses and then with counting. Have the children guess the number of girls present, boys present, and children present. Use counting to verify.

Children realize the value of counting to give precise answers.

They have an opportunity to make educated guesses concerning number and to use counting to check their estimates.

Counting with understanding is reinforced.

Children have an opportunity to use logic.

How many people live in your house?

How many rooms do you think there are in your house?

How many doors are in your house?

Count when you are home to see if your guesses are correct or nearly correct.

From *Hands-On Math*, published by Scott, Foresman and Company, Copyright © 1990 Janet Stone.

Activity 71   Little Porcupines

A picture of a porcupine
Enough clay for each child to make a ball, at least as large as a golf ball (or use dough recipe, page 4)
1 pair of goggly eyes for each child
A box of uncooked spaghetti
A small paper plate for each porcupine to sit on

Discuss porcupines with the children. Show them a picture, pointing out the quills. Tell the children that they may create a porcupine out of clay or dough. Let each child manipulate his clay or dough for a while. If children have trouble coming up with a design they are happy with, suggest that a ball will serve the purpose well. Give each child two goggly eyes to press into his clay or dough where the porcupine's eyes should be.

Next, break spaghetti sticks into 4-in.-long pieces. Let each child push these "quills" into his porcupine, counting aloud every time he adds a quill. He may continue adding quills as long as his counting is accurate. When he skips a number or says an incorrect number, his turn ends and the porcupine has all the quills it needs. For skilled counters, you may need to limit how high they may count!

Have each child press her porcupine onto a paper plate so that it adheres. Write on the plate, "My porcupine has ____ quills!" filling in the blank with the numeral indicating how high the child accurately counted.

My porcupine has 15 quills!

Children gain small motor skill and enjoy creating a "critter" as they practice counting accurately.

They learn about porcupines' having quills.

Porcupines are protected by their quills. Can you think of other animals that have something on their bodies to protect them?

How are bees protected?

How are rattlesnakes protected?

How is a turtle protected?

Fingerpaint numerals in chocolate syrup!
(Activity 78, Sweet Numerals)

Recognizing and Ordering Numerals

THE ACTIVITIES IN THIS SECTION help children identify and recognize numerals and, in some cases, begin writing and ordering them. These skills are useful only if children understand the number or quantity each written numeral symbolizes. Therefore, the activities in this section should be interspersed with activities found in "Counting with Understanding." The goal is not to have children call out numeral names correctly or to write numerals perfectly, but to understand the meaning of each numeral they learn to recognize and be able to use that understanding to create sets, compare sets, use tools such as money and clocks, and further manipulate number.

In the "Counting with Understanding" section, Activities 52 and 53 (Table of 1 and Table of 2) demonstrate an effective way to present a numeral and its meaning for the first time. The activities in this section reinforce numeral recognition by encouraging visual memory through the use of all the senses.

Activity 72   Pretzel Numerals

(send home Parent Note 5)
Pretzels (enough for 12 to 14 children)

       1 package of yeast
       1-1/2 cups warm water
       1/8 teaspoon ginger
       1 teaspoon salt
       1 tablespoon sugar
       4 cups flour

Mixing bowl
Waxed paper, lightly floured
A lightly greased cookie sheet
1 egg, beaten
Coarse salt
An oven

Write the ingredients and the recipe on a large chart or on the chalkboard, so children can see how numerals help us measure and cook. Give each child a job in the cooking process.

Have the children wash their hands. Let children dissolve the yeast in the warm water in a mixing bowl. Next, have them stir in the ginger, regular salt, and sugar, and blend in the flour. Stir the dough until moist and knead it on floured waxed paper until smooth. Break the dough into 12 to 14 pieces and give a piece to each child. Let each child work on a piece of lighly floured waxed paper at a table. Have the children knead the dough a bit more and then roll their dough into ropes that can be shaped into numerals.

Write the numerals you have taught on the board and have the children try to copy them in the air with their arms and hands, pointer fingers extended. Next, let each child try to make one or more of the numerals with his dough. Remind the children that, if they wish to redo a numeral, they can easily roll the dough back into a rope and start again.

When the children are satisfied with their numerals, let them arrange the numerals on the greased cookie sheet and brush the tops with beaten egg (to hold the salt). Let the children sprinkle coarse salt on top of their numerals. Bake at 425°F for 15 minutes. When the pretzels are cool enough to handle, let the children hold up their numerals, announce the names of the numerals, and eat them! Send the recipe home for parents (included in Parent Note 5).

From *Hands-On Math*, published by Scott, Foresman and Company, Copyright © 1990 Janet Stone.

Children see that numbers and numerals help us follow a recipe.

Small motor skills are enhanced as children knead the dough and create numerals.

Children learn to do "air writing" to get a feel for numeral formation.

Children enjoy a tasty snack they made themselves and have a language experience as they share the recipe with parents.

Activity 73   Wax-Resist Numerals

1 white wax candle, large enough to write with
1 white piece of paper for each child
Tempera paint, very watered-down
1 paint brush for each child

Use the white candle to write a large numeral (which you have taught) in the center of each white paper. Press hard as you write the numeral, to leave a wax build-up! Children do not notice the white wax numerals against the white background.

Provide watered-down paint for the children (any color except white). Paint *must* be thin. As the children paint over their papers, the wax resists the paint and children discover numerals suddenly emerging from the painted background! Let each child hold up her paper when dry and identify the numeral that appeared. Label the paper "Wax-Resist Painting."

Children discover that wax resists paint and that candles are made of wax.

Numeral recognition is reinforced.

A painting experience is provided.

Observation skills are sharpened.

How do you think the numeral on your paper got there?

Why didn't you see it before you painted? [Explain that the white waxy candle pushed off the paint (resisted it) and remained uncovered.]

Crayons have wax in them. Let's color pictures and designs with crayons and paint over them to see what happens. (Provide crayons, watered-down paint, and paper. Have the children press hard with crayons.)

Activity 74   Sand Numerals

(send home Parent Note 6)
Index cards for each child, with one large numeral written on each card
Glue in squeeze bottles
Sand

Give each child a set of numeral cards that contains the numerals you have presented in class. Let each child trace over each numeral with his pointer finger to get a feel for its shape. Next, let each child squeeze glue over each line of each numeral, tracing the numeral with the glue. Have each child gather a handful of sand and sprinkle the sand over the glue lines. Let the cards dry for a few hours or overnight. Have each child shake off the excess sand over the trash can and see and feel the sand numeral left behind. Play a game in which children, with their eyes closed, feel numeral cards and guess the identity of numerals without looking. Send the cards home so children can play the game with their parents.

Note: For more interesting sand numerals, color the sand first. Let each child have a small paper cup, half-filled with sand. Add a few drops of food coloring and let each child stir her sand with a popsicle stick until the sand is colored. (At first, the coloring forms tiny clumps. Have the child keep stirring and the color will blend with the sand.) Let the sand dry overnight before sprinkling it on over the glue.

This visual and tactile experience helps children with numeral recognition.

The take-home cards, involving parents, reinforce the learnings.

Small motor skills and eye–hand coordination are enhanced.

How do your sand numerals feel?

Have you ever felt sandpaper? How does it feel? (Pass some sandpaper around, if possible.)

Why does sandpaper have to be rough?

From *Hands-On Math*, published by Scott, Foresman and Company, Copyright © 1990 Janet Stone.

Activity 75   Card Match

55 colored cubes or small blocks
1 or more decks of playing cards

Make 10 towers of cubes, the first having 1 cube, the second having 2 cubes, the third having 3 cubes, and so on, through 10. Provide playing cards with numerals through 10 on them (cover the A for ace with a numeral 1). Have the children count the cubes and sort the playing cards by making a pile of all suits of 3 in front of the tower with 3 cubes, a pile of all suits of 4 in front of the tower with 4 cubes, and so on. As one child completes the sorting (like "dealing"), pile all the cards together, shuffle them, and let another child sort the cards by dealing them to the appropriate towers again. Later, mix all the cubes together and reverse the process, leaving the cards in sorted numeral piles and having the children create towers of cubes to match each card pile's numerals.

Numeral recognition, matching of numerals to concrete sets, and matching of sets to numerals are reinforced.

Children enjoy using playing cards and building block towers.

Numerical ordering and sorting skills play a part in the activity.

Activity 76   Four Corners (for 4s, 5s, and 6s)

A room with four corners that children can stand near
4 numeral signs: 1, 2, 3, 4
A chair in the center of the room

After presenting the numerals 1–4, play the Four Corners game. Each of the four corners of the room is labeled with a sign showing that it is Corner 1, Corner 2, Corner 3, or Corner 4. A caller sits in a chair in the center of the room, and all the other children stand in any of the four corners to begin the game.

The caller closes her eyes and calls out, "Change corners!" Children move to a new corner (encourage children to move quietly, perhaps on tiptoe, so the caller will not hear the direction of anyone's movement). The caller, still with her eyes closed, calls out any corner number, for example, Corner 2. Then she opens her eyes to see who has been caught. Everyone in Corner 2 sits down in the center of the room, around the caller's chair. The caller closes her eyes, calls out "Change corners," and those still in the game move to new corners again. The caller calls out a corner, such as Corner 1, and looks to see who has been caught in Corner 1. The children there join the previously caught children in the center of the room.

The game continues until all the children have been caught and eliminated, except for one; this child is the winner and he becomes the caller for the next game of Four Corners!

Children love this fast-paced game that reinforces numeral recognition, good sportsmanship, auditory skills, large motor skills, and the ability to follow directions.

This is a good introduction to competitive games because the game ends quickly, giving opportunities to "try again."

The nature of the game encourages children to move quickly but quietly and orderly.

Activity 77   Listen and Count

1 numeral card for each child (an index card with a numeral on it that you have presented)
A whistle
A drum
Any other ways to make sounds

Pass out one numeral card to each child. Have each child look at his card and be aware of the numeral. Have the children listen as you clap, counting softly to themselves. When you have finished clapping, for example, 4 times, all the children having a 4 numeral card hold it up. When you clap 8 times, for example, children having cards that say 8 on them hold them up. If someone holds up an incorrect answer, clap again slowly, and have the class count aloud to allow for change of mind! When everyone has had a chance to hold up a numeral, have the children trade cards.

Continue the game by blowing the whistle instead of clapping. When you blow 3 times, the cards with 3 on them are held up and so on. When everyone has had a chance to hold up a card after counting whistle blows, have the children trade cards again.

From *Hands-On Math*, published by Scott, Foresman and Company, Copyright © 1990 Janet Stone.

Continue the game by beating a drum. Continue to have children
listen, count, and hold up numeral cards. Get the children's suggestions for other ways to make sounds to count!

Leave the drum out for children to play with after the activity.

This activity encourages careful listening, auditory memory, and
concentration.

It reinforces numeral recognition and the ability to match numerals
with sets.

I am happy to share my drum with you. Can anyone guess why I
cannot share the whistle? Why should mouth toys not be shared?

What are some toys that can be shared in our classroom? Which are
more fun when used by more than one person at a time?

Is it a good idea to share a toothbrush or a comb? Why not?

Activity 78   Sweet Numerals

Chocolate syrup in a squeeze bottle
Fingerpaint paper for each child

Have the children wash their hands. Pass out a piece of fingerpaint
paper to each child. Let each child squeeze out a puddle of chocolate
syrup on her paper. Encourage children to spread the puddle out by
moving it with a finger, as with fingerpainting. The shiny, dark syrup
stands out from the paper. Children try to form numerals in the syrup,
perhaps as you write some on the chalkboard. Encourage the children
to "erase" numerals (by rubbing over them with their fingers) and
then to make new ones in the syrup. Stress that it is acceptable to lick
fingers because this medium is *not* paint but chocolate! Children enjoy
this form of numeral writing because it smells good, tastes good, looks
good, and feels slippery! When the children tire of making numerals,
encourage them to create shapes, designs, or pictures with the syrup.

The syrup takes a long time to dry. Papers may be covered with plastic
wrap, if you wish to send them home. Use leftover syrup to make
chocolate milk for snack!

Children thoroughly enjoy this multisensory experience that allows them to practice forming numerals and be creative in one activity.

Activity 79   Giant Follow-the-Dots (for 5s and 6s)

Large dots, cut from construction paper
Numeral signs from 1 to 5
Masking tape

Arrange dots and numeral signs to form a follow-the-dot pattern on the floor or a flat carpet. Let the children, working in pairs, take turns following the dots by unrolling and sticking the masking tape from one dot to the next. When a dot pattern is complete, have all of the children stand back and identify it. Use the patterns below or design your own patterns. Patterns do not have to form geometric shapes or pictures; even abstracts or zigzags are fun to walk along to music after completion.

Some suggested patterns:

Triangle	Star
1 3 2	2 4 5 1 3
Square	**Diamond**
1 4 2 3	1 2 4 3

Children experience teamwork and large motor exercise and enjoy music.

Shape recognition, numeral recognition, numerical sequence, eye–hand coordination, and tracking are reinforced.

From *Hands-On Math*, published by Scott, Foresman and Company, Copyright © 1990 Janet Stone.

Follow-Up

Playsheet 17

Follow-the-Dots

Provide each child with a pencil and a copy of Playsheet 17.

Activity 80

Book Pages (for 5s and 6s)

1 book (with clearly numbered pages) for each child in the class (kindergarten primers may be used)
Large numeral signs to hold up

Give each child a book. Have the children look through their books to find where the pages are numbered. As you hold up each numeral sign, ask the children to name the numeral and find the corresponding page in their books. When they find the page number you are holding up, have them hold up that page for all to see.

Let the children look through their books to find the page with the lowest numeral, the highest numeral, a numeral they would like to learn the name of, and so on. This will help the children realize that the same 10 numerals can be used to write larger and larger numerals.

If the books used are not "reading group" books, allow time for the children to look at pictures or "read" the books.

Children see the usefulness of numerals and discover that we can recognize numerals, even if they are written slightly differently in printed material.

Numerical sequence and numeral names are reinforced.

Why do books need page numbers?

How do page numbers help readers?

How many pages do you think would be in a very short book?

How many pages would be in a very long book?

Activity 81   How Many Raindrops?

A bag of cottonballs
Glue
1 sheet of construction paper for each child
A pen or pencil
Blue tempera paint
1 clean eyedropper for each child (sent in by parents or purchased at a pharmacy)
Margarine tubs to hold the paint

Let the children spread and fluff cottonballs to look like clouds, and glue them near the top of their papers. Above each child's cloud, write a numeral she has learned and explain that this indicates how many raindrops will fall from her cloud.

Show the children how to put paint in an eyedropper by squeezing the bulb, and how to release a drop of paint by squeezing again. Let the children make the appropriate number of raindrops under their clouds. Suggest that drops be spaced out, so they won't run together. Have spare paper ready. Once children start making drops, they won't want to stop! Children can make pretty drop pictures with additional paint colors on an extra sheet of paper. (Wash out droppers right after using them. Children will enjoy helping with this, especially at a tub or bowl of water.)

Numeral recognition is reinforced.

Discoveries about air and suction are made as children use the eyedroppers.

Counting with accuracy is encouraged.

There is opportunity for creative art.

Activity 82   Numbered Pockets

Numeral cards, 1–12
A shoe bag (the kind with 12 pockets)
Items to count out and place in the pockets (i.e., straws, clothespins, checkers, popsicle sticks, paintbrushes, colored cubes)

From *Hands-On Math*, published by Scott, Foresman and Company, Copyright © 1990 Janet Stone.

After you have presented many numerals, place one numeral you have taught on each pocket of a shoe bag. Provide items for the children to place in the pockets, creating sets of the number the pocket's numeral indicates.

Later reverse the activity. Have sets of items in each pocket and let the children count the items and label each pocket with the appropriate numeral. (Numeral cards may be placed in the pocket or attached to the outside with a clothespin or paper clip.)

Children gain experience in creating sets of a given number and numbering sets that have already been created.

Numeral recognition and eye–hand coordination are reinforced.

Activity 83   Button Cards

Glue
Assorted buttons (sent in by parents)
Index cards
A marker

Glue a set of buttons on each card, starting with a set of 1 and going as high as the numerals you have taught. On the back of each card, use a marker to write the number of buttons on the other side.

Show the cards, button-side up, on the table to the children. Children count to see the number of the set on each card, then turn the card over to check their counting.

The 5s and 6s enjoy working in pairs, with one child facing another. One child holds up the card, seeing the "secret numeral," and the other counts buttons to discover it!

Children enjoy a guessing game.

They see the usefulness of numerals as they check their answers.

Cooperation is encouraged as children work with partners.

Activity 84 — Tiny Treasure Boxes

TO USE

A container for all the jewels
Small boxes that rings, bracelets, and necklaces come in (the fancier, the better)
A numeral to stick on the top of each box
Small "jewels" to count and place in each box (ask parents to send in old, inexpensive bead necklaces that can be cut apart or buy a bag of beads and spangles at a crafts store)

Note: If the jewels are very small, you may wish to save this activity for children who are at least 4 years old.

TO DO

Place the container of jewels and all the treasure boxes on the table. Stick the numerals on top of each treasure box. Let the children count out the appropriate number of jewels for each box (indicated by the numeral on the lid). Children love handling the tiny treasures, closing and opening the lids, checking one another's counting, and so on. Boxes may be lined up in numerical order after they are filled.

TO BE GAINED

Counting with understanding, numeral recognition, numerical order, eye–hand coordination, and small motor skills are reinforced.

Activity 85 — Bumpy Bugs

TO USE

2 Styrofoam egg cartons or more
Glue
12 goggly eyes or more
Pipe cleaners (to be cut into at least 12 antennae)
Numeral signs, 1–6

TO DO

Cut the bottoms of the egg cartons apart so that you have 1 bump, 2 bumps attached in a line, 3 bumps attached in a line, and so on, through 6 bumps attached in a line. Glue two goggly eyes to the front bump on each line of bumps and push two pipe-cleaner antennae into the head of each bug above the eyes.

From *Hands-On Math*, published by Scott, Foresman and Company. Copyright © 1990 Janet Stone.

Place the bumpy bugs on a table. Have the children count the bumps
on each bug and place the appropriate numeral sign in front of each
bug. Bugs and numerals may then be placed in numerical order.
Children discover that each bug increases in length and that the higher
the number of bumps, the longer the bug.

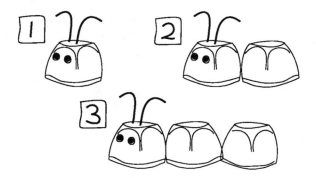

For older children, more bumps may be stapled to bump strips to
make longer and bumpier bugs! Each child may bring in egg cartons
and create bugs of any number of bumps. Children may glue numerals
to the bumps, in order.

Numeral recognition and counting with understanding are reinforced.

Children gain experience in ordering by length and by number.

Follow-Up

Playsheet 18

Fingerprint Bugs

Provide stamp pads, markers, and Playsheet 18 for each child. Children make and count fingerprint bugs by pressing fingers on the
stamp pads and then onto their papers.

Activity 86   Numbered Obstacle Course

Numeral signs, 1–10 (or as high as you like)
10 obstacles for children to overcome:
  a hula hoop to jump into and out of
  a zigzag path to walk made of masking tape
  a tunnel to crawl through or a table to crawl under
  a rocking chair to rock in
  a mat or rug to roll across
  a large box to sit in and climb out of
  a yardstick or balance beam to walk across
  a large pillow to jump over
  something to step up on and jump down from like a short step-up
  a bell to ring
A treat at the end of the course for each child, such as an apple

Set up the obstacle course before the children arrive.

Hold up the numeral signs and review the numerals 1–10. Let the children try placing them in numerical order on a table or on the floor. Demonstrate how to complete each part of the course and assign a number to each part by giving each a numeral sign. Explain that the signs show the order in which to complete the course and that, after a child has completed steps 1 through 10, he or she will come to the bowl of apples and enjoy one!

Variations: For younger children, have only 5 steps to the course. For 6s, try letting the children go backward through the course, from part 10 to part 1! Try rearranging the numeral signs to change the order of the course.

Children enjoy large motor activities as they follow directions, move in numerical sequence, identify numerals, and complete steps toward a major goal.

Follow-Up   Crazy, Mixed-Up Numerals (4s, 5s, and 6s)

Playsheet 19   Provide each child with a copy of Playsheet 19, scissors, and paste.

From *Hands-On Math*, published by Scott, Foresman and Company, Copyright © 1990 Janet Stone.

Activity 87

Fishy Numerals

Fish, cut from poster board or index cards (see Playsheet 20 for a pattern)
A large pail
A small fishing pole or a stick with a string
A magnet, to tie to the end of the string or fishing line
Paper clips, one attached to each fish
Tuna fish and crackers (optional)

On each fish, write a numeral that you have taught the class. Place the fish in the pail and invite the children to go fishing with the fishing pole. (Remember to tie the magnet onto the fishing line.) When the line drops in, the magnet will attract a paper clip and the child will pull in his catch. The child then reads his numeral to the rest of the class; a friend may help, if necessary. For older children, see who catches the biggest numeral!

When all the fish are caught, let the children arrange them in numerical order on the table. Have tuna fish on crackers for snack and talk about how animals provide food for people!

Children see how magnets work while they enjoy a fishing game.

Small motor skills, numeral recognition, and understanding of number size are increased.

Children begin to see how "chance" affects games.

Follow-Up

Fish on a String (for 5s and 6s)

Playsheet 20

Provide each child with scissors, string, and a copy of Playsheet 20. Provide hole punchers to share.

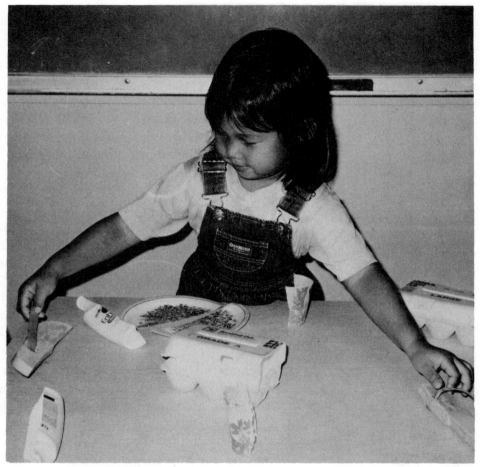

Match halves of things that have been cut apart.
(Activity 89, Bag of Halves)

Parts and Wholes

THE ACTIVITIES IN THIS SECTION provide an awareness of wholes and the parts that make them up. Children enjoy taking things apart and putting them back together again. As they manipulate parts of cars, faces, household items, and even their names, they experience joining and separating, activities that are basic to adding and subtracting, multiplying and dividing. Fractions are introduced, as children play with halves and fourths.

From *Hands-On Math*, published by Scott, Foresman and Company, Copyright © 1990 Janet Stone.

Activity 88   Face Sandwiches

A mirror
1 paper towel for each child
1 slice of bread for each child
Cream cheese or peanut butter
1 popsicle stick for each child
Carrot circles for noses
Olives with pimentos in them (sliced to look like eyes)
Carrot semicircles for ears
Raisins to be lined up for a mouth
Parsley for hair

Encourage each child to look at her face in the mirror, noting all the features and their positions. Discuss the number of eyes, noses, mouths, ears, and so on, that we all have.

Have the children wash their hands. Give each child a paper towel on which to work. Pass out the bread slices. Have each child spread cream cheese or peanut butter on his bread with a popsicle stick. Place all the face parts, which have been washed and sliced ahead of time, on the table.

Children use the foods to create a face. Emphasize that we each look different, so created faces do not have to look the same, but each face should contain all the parts a face needs. After each child creates a face and shows it to the class, let the children eat the face sandwiches for snack or lunch.

Children gain experience with using parts to create a whole.

They see that many small parts may be needed to create 1 whole: just as 2 items are part of a set of 5 items, 1/4 is part of 1, and 2 items plus 4 items make a set of 6 items.

Children also focus on face parts and number, as they think about 2 eyes, 1 nose, and so on.

Similarities and differences in faces are also explored.

The activity results in a nutritious snack.

Follow-Up

Playsheet 21

Make a Face!

Provide each child with glue, cut-up yarn for hair, and a copy of Playsheet 21. Cut out many eyes, noses, mouths, and ears from magazine pictures and have them available on the table. When the children glue parts from various pictures together to form faces, there are some very interesting results!

Activity 89

Bag of Halves

Anything you can easily cut in half (a paper plate, a paper cup, an egg carton, an empty, clean shampoo bottle, an empty cereal box, a toothpaste box)
A large grocery bag

Make a Bag of Halves by cutting all of the items in half and placing all the halves in the grocery bag. Children empty the contents of the bag onto the floor and place matching halves together.

Children discover that 2 halves make a whole.

They match halves and begin to visualize wholes as made up of parts.

Activity 90

Plate Halves

10 or more large, thin paper plates
Markers
Scissors

In the center of each paper plate, draw a shape that can be cut into symmetrical halves and color it in with markers. Cut each paper plate down the middle, so that the shape in the center is cut into two symmetrical halves. Scramble all the halves on the table. Have the children find matching halves and place them together to complete the shape in the center of each plate.

For 5s and 6s, the plates may be cut into fourths. Scramble the fourths, and let the children make the shapes whole again by placing them together on the table.

From *Hands-On Math*, published by Scott, Foresman and Company. Copyright © 1990 Janet Stone.

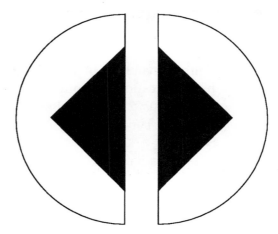

 TO BE GAINED

The concepts of halves and fourths are introduced.
Children see that 2 halves or 4 fourths make 1 whole.
Shape recognition, and matching and visual discrimination skills are reinforced.

Follow-Up

Playsheet 22

Shape Puzzles

Provide each child with a sheet of construction paper, paste, and shape puzzle pieces from Playsheet 22.

Activity 91

Car Parts

 TO USE

Pictures from magazines of cars, trucks, vans, and any other transportation vehicles
Glue
Poster board
Scissors
A large bag

 TO DO

Gather many magazine pictures of vehicles. Mount these with glue to the poster board before cutting closely around their outlines. Cut each vehicle into two parts. Place all the parts in the bag. Children take turns emptying out the vehicle parts, and matching parts that go together.

 TO BE GAINED

Children again see that wholes are made up of parts.

They use visual discrimination and matching skills to create wholes from parts.

Activity 92   Parts to Wholes

Pairs of matching objects (2 Band-Aids, 2 plastic forks, 2 balloons, 2 birthday candles, 2 cotton swabs, 2 leaves of the same type, 2 identical paper cups, 2 dog biscuits)
16 plastic sandwich bags
Scissors
Possibly a hammer!

For each pair of matching objects, place 1 whole object in a plastic sandwich bag. Place the mate in another sandwich bag, after cutting it into many parts. For example, place a whole Band-Aid in one sandwich bag; in another sandwich bag, place all the parts of a Band-Aid you have cut into about 4 pieces. Place a whole plastic fork in a sandwich bag, and in another sandwich bag, place the other fork, after you have broken the tines off; include all the parts in the second sandwich bag. The game will be ready when every item appears whole in one bag and in parts in another bag.

Let the children play a matching game with the bags. Ask the children to place each bag of parts with the bag containing the same item as a whole. Children match a paper cup cut into many pieces with a whole paper cup, a broken-up dog biscuit with a whole dog biscuit, and so on.

Children see the parts that make up wholes.

They match wholes to parts.

The concept of parts making up wholes is reinforced.

Have you ever had something you liked very much that broke apart?

What was done to fix it?

Some toys come in parts and people enjoy putting them together, like model airplanes and puzzles. Can you think of others?

What foods come whole that we take or cut apart? (tangerines, pizza, pie, etc.)

From *Hands-On Math*, published by Scott, Foresman and Company, Copyright © 1990 Janet Stone.

Activity 93   Parts Bag

1 part from various objects such as: a leaf (part of a plant), a page (part of a book), a spinner (part of a game), a pocket (part of a pair of pants), a buckle (part of a belt), a button (part of a shirt), a zipper (part of a dress), the comics page (part of a newspaper), a turning handle and cover (part of a pencil sharpener), a dial (part of a broken clock), a handle (part of a lunchbox)

Place all the parts in a bag. Ask a child to take one part out of the bag and try to guess what whole thing it is a part of. Accept incorrect answers that make sense (a zipper may really be from a dress but "pants" would be an acceptable answer as well). Continue until everyone has had a chance.

Children use logic, visual memory, and imagination to guess the sources of parts.

The concept of wholes being made up of parts is reinforced.

Activity 94   Name Puzzles

(send home Parent Note 7)
A marker
1 large paper plate for each child
Scissors

Using a marker, write a child's name in large letters across a large paper plate. Cut the plate apart, leaving each letter intact, to create a puzzle that the child can put together to recreate her name. For 3s, who may just be learning to recognize their names, you may wish to only cut the name in two parts:

For older children, cut the name into more parts:

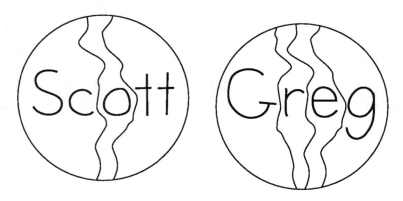

Cuts may be curved or zigzagged, to provide placement clues, or made straight to increase the difficulty:

At first, give each child his own puzzle to work on. Later, you may want to mix many name puzzles on one table, and see who can find her own name parts.

For 6s, let the children try to complete their own name puzzles and other children's puzzles as well. Send home each child's name puzzle with Parent Note 7.

TO BE GAINED

The activity encourages name recognition.

Children use logic, visual memory, and shape matching to make wholes out of parts.

The concept of wholes being made up of parts is reinforced.

From *Hands-On Math*, published by Scott, Foresman and Company, Copyright © 1990 Janet Stone.

Join sets of balloons to make a big set; then each child in the class can receive a balloon.
(Activity 96, Balloon Sets)

Joining and Separating Sets

I N THIS SECTION, *primarily designed for 5s and 6s*, children begin to develop an understanding of addition and subtraction as they join items to form sets of greater number or separate items to form sets of smaller number. They manipulate materials such as peanuts, toothpicks, bottle tops, and marbles to create, join, and separate sets.

Activity 95 Addition Soup

(send home Parent Note 8 a few days before this activity)
Soup ingredients (i.e., carrots, celery, green beans, potato)
A large pot and a ladle
Water
Seasonings and bouillon cubes
A stove or electric burner
A disposable bowl and spoon for each child

Clear a table or shelf on which to accumulate the soup ingredients as they are sent in. Children will see the set of ingredients grow larger as each item is added. When you are ready to make the soup, point out that there is a set of, for example, 1 carrot, plus a set of 2 celery stalks, plus a set of 10 green beans, plus a set of 1 potato, and so on.

Let each child wash his contribution in the sink. Cut up all the vegetables and fill the pot about halfway with water. Let each child add his contribution to the pot, one at a time, pointing out that all the ingredients are joining together in the pot, to make one big pot of Addition Soup. Add seasonings and bouillon cubes, and cook until vegetables are no longer firm.

Serve the soup for snack or lunch. As the children enjoy the soup, encourage them to note the many vegetables found in their bowls. Point out that, even though each child brought in only one vegetable, everyone has many because all the vegetables were joined or added together. When we add things together, we get more!

Children prepare and eat a nutritious snack.

They see how heat and water change things.

They see how joining items together creates a larger set.

Self-worth is increased as each child makes an important contribution to the pot!

How have the vegetables changed during cooking?

Can you still see the item you brought in for the soup?

Would our soup taste the same without your ingredient?

From *Hands-On Math*, published by Scott, Foresman and Company, Copyright © 1990 Janet Stone.

We are all alike in some ways and different in others. Some like soup and some do not. Do you like the soup? What is your favorite ingredient? What is your least favorite?

Follow-Up

Have each child wash her bowl and dry it. Place magazine pictures of vegetables on the table, along with paste. Let the children paste many soup ingredients in their bowls, adding as many as they like, to make a take-home Addition Soup!

Activity 96

Balloon Sets

2 hula hoops or other large rings
1 balloon for each child in the class, some red and some blue

Lay out the two hoops, side by side, on the floor. Tell the children that the hoops will help you tell a make-believe story: One day I went on a walk and found a blue balloon tree! Instead of flowers, blue balloons hung from the branches! The wind suddenly blew all the balloons to the ground. I gathered them up, and here they are (place the blue balloons in one hoop). I hoped there would be enough balloons to pass out to my class. I counted them (count the blue balloons aloud) and found there were only 5; since there are 12 children in my class, I knew I did not have enough balloons, so I saved them.

The next day, I left my house to drive to school, but I saw lots of clouds and thought it was about to rain. Suddenly, instead of raindrops, red balloons began to fall from the clouds. Here they are (place the red balloons in the empty hoop). I counted them (count the red balloons aloud), but found I had only 7; since we have 12 children in our class, I knew I did not have enough red balloons.

What shall I do? I would like to give each of you a balloon, but there are not enough balloons in either hoop. Does anyone have a suggestion that will give our story a happy ending?

Children will suggest passing out both piles of balloons or putting the balloons together. Reword the suggestions: "Good idea! Let's join the two sets of balloons together into one big pile or set." Push the hoops so that one "piles" on top of the other and push the balloons together into one pile inside the hoops. Say, "Now let me see if five balloons and seven balloons together will give us enough balloons for the whole class." Count the balloons aloud, and say, "Five balloons and seven balloons give us twelve balloons, all together." Pass out the balloons, one to each child.

Children are introduced to the idea that sets can be joined, resulting in one larger set.

As balloons are passed out, the concept of one-to-one correspondence is reinforced.

As children listen to a story, auditory skills are emphasized, and logic is used as children suggest solutions.

Follow-Up

Raisin Sets (for 5s and 6s)

Give each child two napkins, placed side by side. Give each child, for example, 2 raisins on one napkin and 1 raisin on the other napkin. Tell the children that, to discover how many they have all together, they can count the raisins as they place them all, 1 at a time, in their hand. When they find the sum, they eat their raisins! Continue having the children create 2 small sets, join them in their hand, count the sum, and eat them for snack!

Activity 97

Peanut Addition (for 5s and 6s)

A bag of unsalted, roasted peanuts
A spinner with the numerals 1–5
1 paper cup for each child
A large bowl in which to pour the peanuts
A blender
1 tablespoon oil
Food on which to spread the peanut butter (crackers, celery sticks, bananas)
Popsicle sticks for spreading

Tell the class that they will be making peanut butter from peanuts for snack today! Each child will be needed to shell the peanuts. Have the children wash their hands.

Give each child a turn to use the spinner. If the spinner lands on 2, for example, the child announces 2 and takes 2 peanuts out of the bowl, placing them in her cup. The child spins again, announces her new number, for example, 3, and adds 3 peanuts to those already in her cup. She then pours her cup's contents on the table and counts to see how many peanuts there are.

Write the resultant equation on the board: 2 peanuts plus 3 peanuts equals 5 peanuts! $2 + 3 = 5$. Be sure to read the equation aloud to the class. Have the child shell the 5 peanuts and place them in a large bowl.

From *Hands-On Math*, published by Scott, Foresman and Company, Copyright © 1990 Janet Stone.

When all the children have added peanuts and shelled them, put the peanuts into the blender with the oil. Blend until peanut butter is formed (for a large class with lots of peanuts, add more oil). Let each child spread peanut butter on a cracker, banana, or celery stick with a popsicle stick.

Counting with understanding and numeral recognition are employed.

Children see that joining sets can result in a larger set.

Addition and equals signs are introduced.

Small motor skills are strengthened as children shell peanuts.

Science discoveries are made as children see the peanuts in the shell, out of the shell, and changed after blending.

All of the senses are used for observation as children see the peanuts, feel them, hear the blender changing them, smell and taste the peanut butter.

Activity 98 Jollypops! (for 5s and 6s)

1 long lollipop stick (available at candy-making stores) or a thin coffee stirrer for each child
Seedless green grapes
Seedless red grapes

Have the children wash their hands. Give each child a stick or stirrer and 2 green grapes. Ask the children to skewer these onto the sticks or stirrers, shish kebab fashion. Next, pass out 3 red grapes to each child. Ask the children to skewer these grapes also. Write the equation 2 + 3 = on the board. Explain as you point to the parts of the equation, "2 green grapes plus 3 red grapes give us . . .?" Children count all the grapes on their sticks to find the sum. Let a child write a 5 on the board to complete the equation. Let the children eat the grapes on their jollypops. As they remove and eat the grapes, they see the number diminishing, until they reach zero. If the budget allows, pass out more grapes and complete more addition equations!

Children concretely join sets as addition equations are written that show what is happening with symbols.

Children see sets get larger and smaller in number as they eat a nutritious snack.

The skewering of the grapes strengthens eye–hand coordination and small motor skill.

Activity 99

Picks and Cubes (for 5s and 6s)

A large piece of Styrofoam (available in craft stores or found in boxes of packaged merchandise such as stereos, televisions, and so on)
A cutting blade
Masking tape
Toothpicks (at least 10 for each child)

Cut the Styrofoam into cubes with the blade. Give each child a Styrofoam cube, with masking tape separating the top surface into two sections. Provide each child with at least 10 toothpicks. On the chalkboard, write 1. Ask each child to place 1 toothpick in the first section of Styrofoam, standing it straight up in the Styrofoam. Next, add a plus sign and another 1 to the chalkboard, so that it now reads 1 + 1. Tell the children that this means to add another toothpick, this time to the second section of their Styrofoam:

Next, add the equals sign so that the chalkboard reads: 1 + 1 = ___. Ask the children to count all of the toothpicks in their Styrofoam cube to see how many there are. Complete the equation on the chalkboard: 1 + 1 = 2. Read the equation aloud to the class. Have the children remove the 2 toothpicks from their cubes.

Continue making equations and having the children create and solve them with toothpicks. Let the children think up equations for the class to try. Those who can write numerals may write their problems on the board.

Children join sets and find sums as the process is written in the form of an addition equation.

Children see that joining sets of 1 or more results in sets of higher number.

From *Hands-On Math*, published by Scott, Foresman and Company, Copyright © 1990 Janet Stone.

Children have a chance to create their own addition equations and then try them out with toothpicks and cubes.

Activity 100 — It's the Tops! (for 5s and 6s)

Bottle tops and caps, sent in by parents (they need to be smooth-edged so they are safe to touch and deep enough to grip, i.e., shampoo bottle tops, tops to hair spray cans, toothpaste pump tops)

Place all the bottle tops in the middle of the table. Write an addition equation on the board, for example, 2 + 2 = ___. Explain that this is a kind of code that means take 2 bottle tops from the center of the table (have everyone do this), then take 2 more bottle tops and add them to the first 2 (have everyone do this). Explain that now each child has a bigger set of bottle tops; ask the children to count their sets, to see how many they have, all added together. When the children find the answer to be 4, write 4 on the board to complete the equation.

Continue to present addition problems and to have the children solve them, using the bottle tops.

Children use concrete objects to solve written addition equations.

They see how to duplicate a written equation in concrete form.

Follow-Up — Dot Addition (for 5s and 6s)

Playsheet 23

Provide a regular-sized pencil with a round eraser at one end for each child. Provide many stamp pads for the class and a copy of Playsheet 23 for each child. Provide scissors and paste for children who cannot write numerals.

Activity 101 — Marble Math (for 5s and 6s)

10 baby food jars (labels removed) and their lids
2 sets of small numerals, 1–5
30 marbles
1 margarine tub for each child (or a produce tray)
Paper and pencil for each child (if the children can write equations)

Label the baby food jars or their lids with the numerals so that you have 2 sets of jars numbered 1–5. Let the children help you place the appropriate number of marbles in each jar and replace the lids. Next, using the marble jars, let a child complete an equation you write on the chalkboard, for example, $3 + 2 = $ ___. The child finds a 3 marble jar and a 2 marble jar and pours out their contents into his margarine tub. He counts all the marbles, and answers 5. Complete the written equation on the board. Let each child solve problems in this way. Each child replaces the marbles in the jars after finding solutions.

If the children are capable, let them have papers and pencils to write equations they discover. Children pour out jars of marbles into their tubs, record the addends, find the sum, and complete the equations.

Children have an opportunity to try joining a variety of sets to discover their sums.

The marbles allow children to see set members join together as they roll into a container.

Children begin to write equations.

Numeral recognition, numeral formation, counting with understanding, and following directions are all reinforced.

Activity 102

People Addition (for 5s and 6s)

Volunteer children to be members of sets

Write a simple addition problem on the board, such as $2 + 1 = $ ___. Ask for two volunteers to stand before the class to represent the 2 in the problem. Explain how the problem shows that we need one more volunteer to stand before the class. When this child comes forward, show how to add all the volunteers together by having them stand close to one another in a line. Ask a child to count all the volunteers to solve the addition problem. When she counts to 3, write the sum of 3 at the end of the addition problem. Continue to solve other addition problems using people as set members.

From *Hands-On Math*, published by Scott, Foresman and Company, Copyright © 1990 Janet Stone.

Practice in joining sets is provided as children complete equations by creating sets with real people.

Children get a feel for addition as they become a part of a set themselves!

Activity 103   Animal Subtraction (for 5s and 6s)

10 stuffed animals
A table
A large box of animal crackers
1 paper towel for each child

Have the children wash their hands for snack time. Arrange the stuffed animals on the table and explain that this is your pet shop. Have a child count the animals, to see how many animals are for sale. Emphasize, after the counting, that you have 10 animals.

Ask a child to pretend to buy a pet and to bring 1 of the animals to his seat. Count the animals in the shop again. Show that now you only have 9. Announce that 10 animals minus 1 animal equals 9 animals, $10 - 1 = 9$.

Ask another child to select and "buy" 2 animals that would like to live together; have the child take the animals to her seat. Count the animals again, emphasizing that 9 animals minus 2 animals leaves (equals) 7 animals. Point out that your stock is getting smaller, that you have fewer animals when any are taken away.

Continue subtracting animals until the pet shop has no animals left. Give each child his own pet shop by placing a set of 4 animal crackers on a paper towel in front of him. Have the children count to tell how many pets are in their shops. Ask the children to eat 1 cracker, then count to see how many pets are left. Continue to eat (subtract) until the pet shops are empty!

Children see that separating sets results in smaller sets.

Children see the meaning of an empty set (zero).

Activity 104   Tasty Subtraction! (for 5s and 6s)

1 paper towel for each child
Soft cream cheese or peanut butter
1 celery stalk for each child, washed
1 popsicle stick for each child
A bag of thin pretzel sticks

Have the children wash their hands. Give each child a paper towel. On it, place enough cream cheese or peanut butter to stuff the celery and a popsicle stick to spread the cream cheese or peanut butter. After each child has filled her piece of celery, pass out about 10 pretzel sticks to each child. Have children count out, for example, 8 sticks, and stand them in the celery "holder."

Write 8 on the board. Next, suggest that the children remove 2 pretzels and eat them. Have the board now read: 8 – 2 = ____. Ask how many pretzels are left standing in the celery. When the children count and answer 6, complete the equation on the board: 8 – 2 = 6. Show how the equation tells what just happened with the pretzels. Have the children place remaining unused pretzels in the celery and count how many sticks are in it. When they answer 8, write 8 on the board. Ask the children to remove 4 and eat them. Have the board now read:
8 – 4 = ____. Ask the children to count to see how many are left standing. When they count and answer 4, complete the equation to read:
8 – 4 = 4.

Continue subtracting pretzels and writing corresponding equations until all the pretzels are eaten! Point out that separating sets results in fewer and that joining sets results in more. Let everyone eat the stuffed celery.

Children are exposed to a written subtraction equation.

They concretely work the equation with pretzel sticks, held in their celery and cream cheese holder.

Children begin to see the opposition of joining and separating sets.

They use eye–hand coordination, small motor skill, counting skills, and numeral recognition as they work equations and eat a nutritious snack.

From *Hands-On Math*, published by Scott, Foresman and Company, Copyright © 1990 Janet Stone.

Activity 105

Lost Gold (for 5s and 6s)

A bag of large lima beans
Old newspaper
A can of gold spray paint
1 paper cup for each child

Spread the lima beans out on newspaper. Spray paint them gold. When one side is dry, turn them over and paint the other side. They dry quickly and look like tiny gold nuggets.

Give each child 10 gold nuggets in a paper cup. Show a subtraction equation, for example, $5 - 2 =$ ___. Have each child take 5 gold nuggets from the cup and line them up on the floor or table. Show how the equation tells us to take away 2 gold nuggets. Have the children place 2 of the 5 on their laps. Ask them to count the remaining nuggets in line to find the difference. When the children answer 3, complete the written equation. Have the children return all gold nuggets to their cups and get ready for the next subtraction equation.

Continue presenting subtraction equations and letting the children solve them with gold nuggets.

Children enjoy using "gold nuggets" to gain practice in solving subtraction equations.

Children separate sets according to written equations and find differences.

Follow-Up

Playsheet 24

Disappearing Act! (for 5s and 6s)

Provide each child with a copy of Playsheet 24. Children subtract rabbits by making them disappear. Provide white shoe polish in applicator bottles to delete rabbits. (White paint on cotton swabs may be used as well.)

Activity 106

Cotton Subtraction

A poster board
A bag of cotton balls
A grasping implement for each child, such as tweezers, tongs, or a spring clothespin (if you have a limited supply, let children take turns)
1 produce tray for each child
A set of numeral cards

From *Hands-On Math*, published by Scott, Foresman and Company, Copyright © 1990 Janet Stone.

Write a number of subtraction equations on the poster board (i.e., 5 − 2 = ___, 6 − 3 = ___, 4 − 1 = ___).

Show the children the poster and explain that they will take turns finding the answers to the subtraction problems by separating sets of cotton balls. Explain that they will not separate the cotton balls directly with their fingers. Instead, they will use the tweezers, tongs, or clothespins to pick up the cotton balls and release them (just for the fun of it, and to add small motor exercise to the activity).

Spread all the cotton balls out on a table. Demonstrate how to work the problem 5 − 2, for example. Using the tweezers, tongs, or clothes-pin, pick up 5 cotton balls, 1 at a time, and release them into the pro-duce tray. Now, according to the problem, take away 2 cotton balls by picking them up with the implement and taking them out of the tray. Next, count the number of cotton balls left in the tray. When 3 is found to be the difference, find the 3 numeral card and place it after the equals sign on the poster board so the equation reads 5 − 2 = 3. Replace all cotton balls on the table. Let children take turns with the cotton subtraction.

Children strengthen small motor skills and understanding of subtraction as a separating of sets.

Activity 107 — Cheerios Abacus (for 5s and 6s)

1 long pipe cleaner for each child
1 Styrofoam cube for each child
10 Cheerios or other loop-shaped cereal pieces for each child
Index cards with addition or subtraction equations for the children to solve

Give each child a long pipe cleaner and a Styrofoam cube. Have each child stand the pipe cleaner in the center of the cube. Give each child 10 cereal rings to thread on the standing pipe cleaner, 1 on top of another. When all 10 rings are piled with the pipe cleaner through their centers, have the children stick the free end of the pipe cleaner into the Styrofoam by bending the pipe cleaner backward to form an arc. Cereal rings will now move forward or backward, along the pipe-cleaner arc.

From *Hands-On Math*, published by Scott, Foresman and Company, Copyright © 1990 Janet Stone.

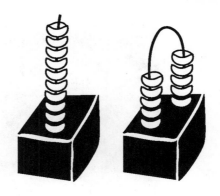

Give each child an equation card. For example, if the equation is
5 – 2 = ___, show the child how to first have 5 cereal rings on the front
of the arc, how to subtract 2 by moving 2 of the 5 rings to the back of
the arc, and finally, how to count the rings that are still left in front to
find the difference of 3. Continue trading equation cards and working
out solutions with the Cheerios abacus.

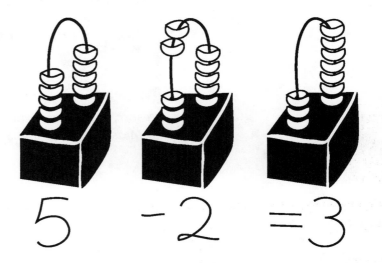

From *Hands-On Math*, published by Scott, Foresman and Company, Copyright © 1990 Janet Stone.

TO BE GAINED

Children enjoy making and using their own abacus.

They see how to use an abacus to separate sets and discover how to
join sets on it as well.

They see that instruments can help us solve mathematical problems.

TO DISCUSS

Do any of your parents have instruments that help them solve number
problems? (If possible, show an adding machine, a calculator, a com-
puter, or any other such tool.)

If we can find answers by counting peanuts or lima beans or Cheerios,
why do we need instruments that solve number problems?

Have you ever seen a receipt from a store's cash register? What does it
show?

Mix, pour, measure, and explore water!
(Activity, 119, Measuring Cups and Spoons)

Tools of Measure- ment

N THIS SECTION, children explore the use of timers, clocks, rulers, coins, balance scales, and measuring cups and spoons. They begin to see the usefulness of these tools as they time the preparation of butter, make a tablecloth, purchase a fudge-pop, compare the weights of objects, and measure ingredients for recipes.

From *Hands-On Math*, published by Scott, Foresman and Company, Copyright © 1990 Janet Stone.

Activity 108   Timed Sharing!

A timer
1 book or toy for each child

Show the timer and elicit responses as to what it is for. Show how we can set it to keep track of passing time and to ring when a certain amount of time has gone by. Explain that a timer keeps track of amounts of time called minutes. Tell the children that a minute is about as long as it takes to count to 60. Let those who can help you count aloud to 60.

Tell the children that the timer will count to 60 for us and ring when a minute is up. Have everyone try not to make a sound for 1 minute. Set the timer for 1 minute, reminding the class to be very quiet until the timer rings, to see how long a minute is.

Tell the class that the timer can keep track of many minutes, all the way up to 60 minutes, or a whole hour! Pass out one book or toy to each child. Tell the children that you will set the timer for 3 minutes and that, until the timer rings, each child may look at his book or enjoy her toy (quietly, so the timer bell can be heard). Explain that when the timer rings, 3 minutes will have passed and it will be time to trade books or toys. Set the timer for 3 minutes and let the "reading" or playing begin. When the timer rings, have each child pass the book or toy to the next child. Repeat the procedure 3 or 4 times, to give the idea of time passing and the timer keeping track.

Use the timer throughout the day. Examples: Set the timer for 5 minutes and explain that, when it rings, it will be time for snack. Set the timer for 30 minutes and bring it to the playgound. When it rings, it will be time to go into the classroom. Set the timer for 4 minutes, and see if the room can be cleaned up by the time the timer rings!

Children become familiar with a timer.

They see one way of keeping track of time.

Children gain an idea of the length of a minute.

Sharing is encouraged, along with an appreciation for books.

Children enjoy trying to beat the timer.

Follow-Up

Timed Marble Roll Painting

Let each child have a turn placing a sheet of white paper inside a shoe box, pressing it down against the bottom and sides of the box. Provide 2 cups of different colors of tempera paint. Let the child drop one marble into each cup so that the marbles get covered with paint. Let the child spoon out each marble, dropping the two marbles onto the paper inside the shoe box. Set the timer for 1 minute and have the child gyrate, shake, and move his arms about while holding the shoe box out in front of him, until the timer rings. During that minute, the marbles will have rolled all about the paper, creating pretty paint tracks everywhere! Drop the marbles back into the paint cups and remove the paper. Label it "Timed Marble Roll."

Activity 109

Finding Time

A timer, with as loud a tick and ring as possible

Show how the timer works (see Activity 108); point out that it ticks until it rings and stops. Have the children hide their eyes while you hide the timer in a place where its tick can still be heard. The children then search for the timer by listening to its ticking and tracking down its location. The object is to find the timer before it rings and time is up. (Be sure to set the timer for a reasonable amount of time.) Perhaps the finder can be the next person to hide the timer.

Children gain a sense of passing time.

Auditory skills are strengthened.

Children become more familiar with a timer and the fact that it rings when a certain amount of time has passed.

They are encouraged to observe carefully.

Activity 110

Using Clocks

As many watches and clocks as possible (with at least one alarm clock and one digital clock)

From *Hands-On Math*, published by Scott, Foresman and Company, Copyright © 1990 Janet Stone.

Display the watches and clocks on the table. Allow some time for children to examine watches and clocks on the table. If possible, provide old or broken clocks on which the children may move the hands. Discuss similarities and differences: Some are electrical, some use batteries, some tick, some have hands and the numerals 1 through 12 while others (digital) do not have hands and have larger numerals.

Explain that, most days, children wake up, eat breakfast, go to school, come home, eat dinner, enjoy the evening, go to bed, and then wake up to a new day. Tell the class that each day has 24 hours in it, and that clocks help us keep track of what part of the day it is, of what hour it is, and of what hour it will be next. Show how, on a traditional clock, there are hands to tell us the name of the time, the name of the present hour. Show that on a digital clock, the name of the time appears in numerals on the face of the clock.

Use a clock that has hands you can move to show how the hour changes. Point out the hour hand and let the children help you call out each hour as the hand moves from 12:00 to 1:00 to 2:00 and so on.

Go through a "pretend day." Turn the hands to 7:00 and have the children pretend to be sleeping. Set the alarm to go off at 7:00 and "wake" the class up. Let them pretend to dress and eat. Make the clock show 8:00 and have everyone pretend to drive in a car to school. Make the clock show 12:00 and everyone pretend to eat lunch. Continue to show events and times until you reach 8:00 A.M. again.

To show how long an hour is, have everyone see where the hands are on a traditional clock at, say, 11:00. Set the alarm to ring at 12:00. When the alarm goes off, point out that a whole hour has gone by. Ask the children to note how the hour hand is pointing to 12 instead of to 11.

Let the children watch a digital clock for a few minutes. They will enjoy seeing the numerals change. It is easier to see minutes go by on a digital clock than on a traditional clock.

Let the children take turns moving the hour hand on a traditional clock and seeing who can guess the name of the hour. Point out that they are learning the first step to telling time!

Children become familiar with clocks, as tools for keeping track of time.

They see how the hands move and how the hour changes.

Numeral recognition is reinforced.

Children enjoy dramatizing daily events.

Follow-Up

Mock Clocks (for 4s, 5s, and 6s)

Provide each child with a paper plate on which you have placed a dot where each hour numeral should be. Also provide glue or paste and the numerals 1 through 12 on paper. Give each child a brad to poke through the center of the paper-plate clock, a long (hour) hand, and a short (minute) hand.

Have the children look at a real clock and paste numerals where they should go on their paper-plate clocks. Let them attach a minute hand and an hour hand to their clocks by fastening the hands to the center with a brad. Children may practice showing various hours of the day on their mock clocks.

Activity 111

Time It!

(send home Parent Note 9)
1/2 pint heavy whipping cream
A baby food jar with a lid
A stopwatch or a watch
Bread or crackers
Popsicle sticks for spreading butter

Tell the class that, with a lot of cooperation, they will make butter out of cream. Pour the cream into the baby food jar, filling about two-thirds of the way, and put the lid on; close tightly. Explain that each child will have a turn to shake the jar up and down until the cream forms into a ball of butter. Ask for guesses (estimates) of how long this will take. Show the stopwatch and explain that it keeps track of how much time passes. Be sure to start it when the shaking begins and to stop it when the butter forms. (If no stopwatch is available, use a watch to calculate how long the process takes.)

Give each child a chance to shake the jar. When the butter forms, announce how long it took; see if any estimates were close. Let the children spread the butter on bread or crackers with popsicle sticks.

Children see that a stopwatch is another tool for keeping track of time.

They learn that butter is made from cream.

They see the advantages of teamwork.

They have a chance to predict how long an activity will take.

From *Hands-On Math*, published by Scott, Foresman and Company, Copyright © 1990 Janet Stone.

Activity 112 — Heavy or Light

A balance scale
5 blocks of the same size
A tissue
A book
A cork
A heavy rock
A dry sponge
A very wet sponge
2 baby food jars
Marbles

Show the class the balance scale. Ask if anyone knows what it is used for. Discuss how it helps us know what is heavier, what weighs more.

Put 1 block on one side of the balance scale. Show how the weight of the block makes that side of the scale go down. Put 4 blocks on the other side of the scale. Ask why that side went lower than the first side. Discuss how 4 blocks of the same size weigh more or are heavier than only 1 block of that size. Move the blocks so that there are 2 blocks on each side of the scale. Show how it balances when both sides weigh the same.

Ask whether the children think the tissue or the book is heavier. Ask how we can find out for sure. Use the balance scale to see which side gets lower—the book side or the tissue side. The book's weight pushes that side down; the book is heavier and the tissue is lighter.

Ask which is probably heavier—the cork or the rock. Ask a child to test this by using the balance scale. By watching what the scale does, ask the child to tell which is heavier and which is lighter.

Ask which is probably heavier—a dry sponge or one filled with water. Have a child test her answer by using the balance scale. Next, wet the dry sponge and wring out the wet sponge. What happens on the scale now?

Compare an empty baby food jar with one filled with marbles. Ask for predictions about what will happen when they are placed on the balance scale. Test out the predictions.

Let the children find two things in the room whose weights they want to compare. Let them tell, by feel, which object is heavier. Let them test their answer by using the balance scale. Allow time for free experimentation with the balance scale.

Children see how balance scales are used to compare weights.

Children see that heavier objects make the scales move lower than do lighter objects.

They learn about concepts of heavy and light, and predict which of two items is heavier.

Follow-Up

Heavier and Lighter

Give each child a paper on which you have drawn two columns. Label one column "Heavier" and one column "Lighter." Give each child a cotton ball to hold in one hand and a small rock to hold in the other hand. Ask which is heavier, which is lighter, and let him use the balance scale to check his answer. Then have him glue each item in the appropriate column on his paper.

Repeat the above process with a feather and a washer, a small piece of Styrofoam and a fishing sinker, and a piece of tin foil (wadded up as a ball) and a metal nut.

Activity 113

Sorting Coins

A collection of pennies, nickels, dimes, quarters, and half dollars
A small bowl to hold all the coins
5 clear plastic cups

Discuss how, in the United States, we use coins or paper money to purchase goods and services. Explain that today the class will be looking at coins of the United States. Show the bowl of coins. Hold up and name the penny, nickel, dime, quarter, and half dollar. Show the 5 plastic cups. Place a penny in one, a nickel in the next, a dime in the next, a quarter in the next, and a half dollar in the last plastic cup. Ask the children to sort the coins in this way, separating them into like piles, until the bowl is empty. See who can name the coins in each cup. Mix all the coins together again in the bowl and let the children take turns sorting them again. This sorting makes the children aware of the similarities and differences in the coins.

Children are introduced to U.S. coins.

They begin to see similarities and differences in the coins and begin to sort them.

What are coins used for?

What other kind of money do we have?

Have you ever bought something with money? Where did you get the money and what did you buy?

Why do many people save money?

Activity 114 — Coin Rubbings (for 4s, 5s, and 6s)

Scotch tape
A collection of pennies, nickels, dimes, quarters, and half dollars
White, thin paper for each child (tracing paper, typing paper)
A pencil for each child

Double-back pieces of Scotch tape so that coins stick to the table-top without taping over them. Show the children how to place their papers over a coin and rub back and forth with a pencil on the papers to create a coin rubbing. Make sure they have opportunities to rub over head and tail sides of coins. This activity makes the children more aware of similarities and differences in coin sizes and pictures. When rubbings are completed, remove the tape from the coins and let the children match the coins to the rubbings by placing coins on top of matching rubbings. See who can point to a penny rubbing, a nickel rubbing, a dime rubbing, and so on. Label the papers "Coin Rubbings" and send them home.

Children become more familiar with coins as they manipulate them to make coin rubbings.

They see and feel differences and similarities.

They begin to learn coin names.

Activity 115 — Treat Shop

2 large boxes of chocolate pudding mix, instant
6 cups of whole milk
Large bowl, mixing spoon
1 small paper cup for each child
1 popsicle stick for each child
Freezer

From *Hands-On Math*, published by Scott, Foresman and Company, Copyright © 1990 Janet Stone.

A price sign
5 pennies for each child (you will get these back!)
1 nickel for each child (you will get these back!)

Tell the children that you are setting up a treat shop that will sell delicious fudge-pops for 5¢ each. Tell them that you will give them each the money they need to shop at the treat shop.

Follow the directions on the pudding mix box to make chocolate pudding; let each child help pour, measure, or stir. When the pudding is made, spoon some into each small cup. Let each child add a popsicle stick to one pudding cup. Freeze these; they become tasty fudgesicles!

When the fudge-pops are ready (perhaps the next day), put them on the table with the price sign that says "Fudge-Pops, 5¢ each." Read it to the class. Explain that since the fudge-pops are 5¢, they will each need 5 pennies to buy one. Give out pennies to the children, 1 at a time, and tell them to tell you when they have enough pennies to purchase a fudge-pop. When all have 5 pennies, ask them to count once again to be sure they have 5¢. Now, ask if anyone would like to trade the pennies for a nickel; explain that a nickel is the same as (is equal to) 5 pennies. Let the children who wish to trade do so. Have all the children hold up their money. Note that they all have 5¢, some in the form of 5 pennies and some in the form of 1 nickel. Let the children trade pennies for nickels with one another. Finally, "sell" the fudge-pops for 5¢ each. Show the children how to peel off the paper cup in order to eat the treat while holding the stick.

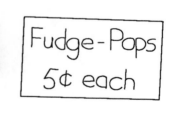

Fudge-Pops
5¢ each

Children enjoy a cooking activity and a nutritious snack.

They see that coins are used to purchase goods and that 5 pennies may be traded for 1 nickel.

They become aware of the "¢" sign and that it symbolizes *cents*.

Activity 116 — Piggy Banks (for 4s, 5s, and 6s)

1 "soft" can with a lid for each child (ready-made icing cans, macaroon cans, round oatmeal boxes)
Paintbrush and paint
Glue

From *Hands-On Math*, published by Scott, Foresman and Company, Copyright © 1990 Janet Stone.

Sand
One 9-ounce, clear plastic cup for each child
1/2 Styrofoam egg carton for each child, preferably pink
Scotch tape
A permanent black marker
Matches
1 penny for each child

Explain that a piggy bank is a good way to save coins until enough money is saved to buy something you want. Money is added until a desired sum is reached.

To make the banks, let each child paint a "soft can," preferably pink. (If the can is plastic, add glue to the paint to make it adhere.) When the can is dry, let each child place some sand in the can (to help it balance later) and glue on the lid. Have each child stand the can upright and add a line of glue to the lid where the cup will meet it when placed mouth-side-down on top. Have the children press the cup to the lid and let dry.

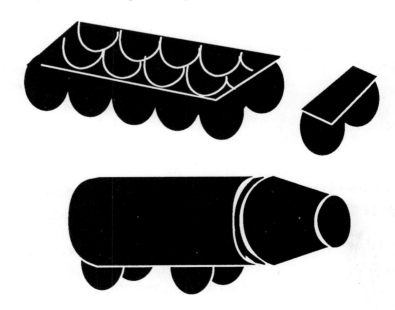

From the egg cartons, cut out the feet, tail, and ears for each child. For the feet, cut out two adjoining egg compartments for the front pair and two adjoining egg compartments for the back pair. Cut out each pair as a unit, instead of cutting them apart, down the middle.

For ears, cut one egg compartment in half, forming two triangular-shaped ears:

For the tail, cut one egg compartment in a spiral fashion, following the shape of the compartment from the outside increasingly toward the center:

The center can be pulled to make the tail springlike:

Give each child a number of strips of cellophane tape, which can be hung off the table's edge until used. Children use these tape strips to attach the ears, feet, and tail in the appropriate places.

slot

Children add nostrils, eyes, and a mouth with the permanent marker.

Use a lighted match to quickly melt a coin slot in each snout (the match makes a neat slit; cutting tends to create cracks). Having the money slot in the snout allows children to see the money as it accumulates. Let each child drop in 1 penny to get her savings started. The sand in the body can be shifted to balance the bank when money makes the front end heavy.

TO BE GAINED

Children become interested in saving money.

They gain small motor skill as they add features to their pigs.

Placement and number of features (2 eyes, 2 ears, 1 mouth) are reinforced.

From *Hands-On Math*, published by Scott, Foresman and Company, Copyright © 1990 Janet Stone.

Children gain pride in creating something useful and attractive.

Recognition of the penny is taught.

TO DISCUSS

What are some things you would like to save up for?

What are some ways you could earn money?

Do some of your parents go to savings banks? What are these for?

Activity 117

Using Rulers (for 4s, 5s, and 6s)

TO USE

Assorted "store-bought" rulers
1 copy of Playsheet 25 for each child
Glue
Cardboard to back Playsheet 25
Scissors
Kraft paper, on the roll
Crayons or markers

TO DO

Let the class examine "store-bought" rulers, discussing what they are and what they think they are used for. Talk about how rulers help us know the size of things, how big, how long, how wide things are. Show how a ruler would help if we needed to make curtains for a window in the classroom.

Pass out Playsheet 25 to each child. Point out that it shows a ruler. Have everyone point to the numerals and say them aloud with you. Explain that each numeral stands for another inch and that all 12 inches make up one unit of measure called a *foot*.

Have each child glue her playsheet to a piece of cardboard; adults will probably need to cut the rulers out. When each child has her ruler cut out, ask for volunteers to line up their rulers down the length of a table to see how many rulers long (how many feet long) it is. Round off the amount, saying something like, "The table is about five feet long; it took five rulers to reach from end to end." Ask if anyone knows how a table can be measured if someone has only one ruler. Let the child show how to move the ruler down the length of the table, keeping track of how many times the whole ruler is used. Have the children help you measure the bookshelves, the doorway, the rug using rulers. Show how to account for extra inches.

Tell the class that you would like to make a tablecloth for today's snack time. Have the children help you measure the table exactly, writing down the number of feet and inches of its length and width.

Unroll a large section of the kraft paper. Measure it and draw cutting lines to the table's length and width. Have the children help you cut it out on the floor. Let children place it on the table and see how well it fits, thanks to measuring. Let the children decorate the tablecloth with crayons or markers and use it at snack time!

Children are exposed to the idea that rulers help us measure length and width in units called inches.

They see that numbers help us keep track of length and width.

They begin to manipulate rulers.

They see how a tablecloth is measured and enjoy an art activity.

Activity 118   Measured Lines (for 5s and 6s)

Cardboard rulers from Activity 117 (Playsheet 25)
1 copy of Playsheet 26 for each child
A pencil for each child

Have children gather near you at the chalkboard (or at a large piece of paper). Show how you use the ruler to create a 2-inch line, a 4-inch line, and so on. Point out that you hold the ruler still, press the chalk or pencil against the side of the ruler as you write, and stop at the numeral 2 or 4. Let each child try to draw a 3-inch line on the chalkboard or paper while you hold the ruler.

Give Playsheet 26 and a pencil to each child. Have the children work in pairs so that one child can hold the ruler still while the other draws his lines. Explain the playsheet's directions.

Children use rulers to make lines of specified length.

They see how rulers measure and let us draw straight lines.

They create a line of a length they choose.

Follow-Up   Line Art

Let the class use the cardboard rulers and other rulers from Activities 117 and 118 to make free drawings. They may discover intersecting lines, parallel lines, angles, and so on.

From *Hands-On Math*, published by Scott, Foresman and Company, Copyright © 1990 Janet Stone.

Activity 119

Measuring Cups and Spoons

A set of measuring cups
A set of measuring spoons
A water tub (a plastic tub for bathing a baby will do)
Water
Food coloring (optional)
Eyedroppers (optional)
Rice
Funnel and scoops (optional)
Containers (such as margarine tubs, plastic cups, 35-mm film containers)

Show the measuring cups and spoons and initiate a discussion about what their purpose is. Set up a "measuring center." Provide the tub, about half-filled with water and the measuring cups and spoons, along with other containers, into which measured water can be poured. Let the children experiment and explore. Food coloring may be added to the water for added interest. Eyedroppers and basters will add to the fun. Children discover many things about the capacity of the cups and spoons as they play.

On another day, have rice in the tub instead of water. A funnel and scoops will add to the fun. (This activity is best done outdoors, as rice inevitably falls on the classroom floor and can cause the children to slip.) Children discover differences in measuring solids versus liquids.

Children see similarities and differences in measuring liquids and solids.

They enjoy using adults' tools and exploring with water and rice.

They see that larger cups hold more water and rice than do smaller cups.

They practice small motor skills as they mix and pour.

Color recognition is reinforced.

Follow-Up

Sand Painting

Have each child use a 1/2-cup measure to collect 1/2 cup of sand from the sandpile. Have her pour the sand into a margarine tub and add 1/8 teaspoon of food coloring to the sand. Let her stir the sand with a popsicle stick. After a good deal of stirring, she will have colored sand.

From *Hands-On Math*, published by Scott, Foresman and Company, Copyright © 1990 Janet Stone.

Children squeeze glue from squeeze bottles in interesting designs onto construction paper. They then sprinkle colors of sand over the glue. When the glue dries, children shake off the excess sand and discover beautiful sand paintings!

Activity 120 Individual Gelatin

1 paper cup for each child
4 bowls
Measuring tablespoon and teaspoon
Packages of gelatin, any flavors
Hot water
1/4-cup measure
1 spoon for each child
1 ice cube for each child
1 banana slice (circle) for each child
Access to a refrigerator

This activity lets each child prepare his own gelatin snack and see the value of using measuring tools. On a table, line up the following, in order:
paper cups
a bowl into which you have poured the packaged gelatin, with a tablespoon and a teaspoon in front of the bowl
a bowl of hot water (show the class how to handle it carefully), with a 1/4-cup measure in front of the bowl
plastic spoons
a bowl of ice cubes
a bowl with banana slices in it

Have the children wash their hands and line up near the table. Explain that the children will move in front of the table, adding ingredients as they go. They first take a cup, then measure a tablespoon *and* a teaspoon of gelatin into the cup (show how to measure a level tablespoon and teaspoon). Next, they add 1/4 cup of water, then stir with a spoon. When the gelatin dissolves, they add one ice cube and stir until it is melted. Finally, they add a banana slice to their cups. Spoons may be rinsed and saved for eating the gelatin. Refrigerate the gelatin until set.

Children see the importance of following directions and progressing in sequential order.

They have an opportunity to use measuring cups and spoons in a purposeful way.

They see gelatin and ice dissolving and discover the effect of refrigeration on the recipe.

They enjoy a snack they made themselves!

Activity 121   Measure Up!

(send home Parent Note 10)
Yarn or string
1 pine cone for each child
1/4-cup and 1/3-cup measures
Popsicle sticks
A large jar of peanut butter
A bag of wild birdseed
1 paper lunch bag for each child

This activity provides an opportunity to use measuring tools and to show kindness to animals! Each child creates a bird feeder to hang in a tree at home.

Before beginning, tie a piece of string or yarn to each pine cone so that the feeder can later be tied to a tree branch. Have each child measure out 1/4 cup of peanut butter and spread it with a popsicle stick onto and into his pine cone, making the pine cone sticky. Next, have each child measure 1/3 cup of wild birdseed and pour this into a lunch bag (one not containing lunch, of course). Have each child drop his sticky pine cone into the bag of seed, close the bag, and shake the bag hard repeatedly. The seeds will stick to the peanut butter and coat the pine cone, resulting in a delicacy for wild birds! After each child peeks at the pine-cone feeder, let him or her take it home in the bag, with Parent Note 10.

Children have a sense of pride as they help wild birds.

They use measuring tools to create a bird feeder and see that it feels good to share.

(After children have had the feeders home for a few days) Has anyone seen any birds at the bird feeder?

Who would like to tell what he or she saw?

Parent Notes

**Parent Note 1
(Activity 11)**

Dear Parents,
The class enjoyed working with puzzles made out of cereal boxes today! Your child is bringing one home. You might enjoy completing the puzzle together, noting the shape names of the puzzle pieces, or watching your child complete the puzzle without any help at all. You may want to create more box puzzles at home.

**Parent Note 2
(Activity 23)**

Dear Parents,
Your child helped make modeling dough at school today and then created big objects and small objects with the dough.

Perhaps you would like to make some modeling dough at home to help your child continue to learn about sizes and to have fun! Here is our recipe:

Add about 5 drops of food coloring to 1 cup of water and mix. Pour this into 3 cups of flour and 1/4 cup of salt. Mix and knead. If it is too sticky, add flour. If it is too dry, add water.

Model with the dough on waxed paper. Store the dough in a plastic bag.

**Parent Note 3
(Activity 37,
Follow-Up)**

Dear Parents,
We are learning about *big* and *small* and differences in size. Please send a baby picture of your child to school and, if possible, a piece of your child's baby clothing. We want to see how small the children used to be and how big they are now!

**Parent Note 4
(Activity 45)**

Dear Parents,
We made delicious orange-juice popsicles at school! The children saw how freezing changes liquids to solids. They also saw that each child has to prepare *one* popsicle in order for each child to eat *one* popsicle later! You may want to make nutritious popsicles at home by freezing juice. Your child can tell you how!

From *Hands-On Math*, published by Scott, Foresman and Company, Copyright © 1990 Janet Stone.

Parent Note 5
(Activity 72)

Dear Parents,
We made hot pretzels in the shape of numerals today! Would you like to try our recipe, and review numeral names and shapes with your child while you have fun? Here's what to do:

Dissolve one package of yeast in 1-1/2 cups warm water in a bowl. Stir in 1/8 teaspoon ginger, 1 teaspoon salt, and 1 tablespoon sugar. Blend in 4 cups flour. Stir until moist and knead on floured waxed paper until smooth. Break the dough into 12 pieces. Have the family members knead the pieces, roll them into ropes, and form numerals with them (or anything else they desire). Place your pretzels on a greased cookie sheet and brush the tops with beaten egg. Sprinkle with coarse salt and bake at 425°F for 15 minutes. Yummy!

Parent Note 6
(Activity 74)

Dear Parents,
Your child made sand numerals in school today! You may want to join your child in a game. Close your eyes and have your child pass you a sand numeral. Try to guess its name without looking, only by touching. Next, let your child feel a numeral and guess its name, without looking at it. Continue taking turns. As you play, your child learns the shapes of numerals by sight and touch.

Parent Note 7
(Activity 94)

Dear Parents,
We played with name puzzles today! Your child will be glad to show you how to join the parts to make a whole name. You can make a puzzle of your last name on a paper plate, if you wish.

Parent Note 8
(Activity 95)

Dear Parents,
We will make Addition Soup on _____. Before that day, please send in _____. (a carrot, a potato, string beans, etc.) Each child will add something to the pot until we have a delicious and nutritious soup that is full of fresh vegetables! The children will discover the advantages of sharing and that joining many items together results in a big set of items.

Thank you for your help!

Appreciatively,

Parent Note 9
(Activity 111)

Dear Parents,
We made butter today! We took turns shaking whipping cream in a closed jar. We shook and shook and shook. Sharing the work was fun. We timed our shaking. It took ___ minutes for the cream to turn to butter. The butter was delicious on bread and crackers.

Parent Note 10
(Activity 121)

Dear Parents,
The children worked hard today to help wild birds. By carefully measuring and spreading peanut butter and by measuring and shaking birdseed, each child created a pine-cone bird feeder! Please help your child complete this project by hanging the feeder in a tree near your home. Your child will enjoy watching the feeder and the happy birds it attracts!

Thank you!

From *Hands-On Math*, published by Scott, Foresman and Company, Copyright © 1990 Janet Stone.

Tracing Shapes

Trace over the outline of each shape with a cotton swab dipped in paint. Decorate the inside of each shape with dots, stripes, or any other design!

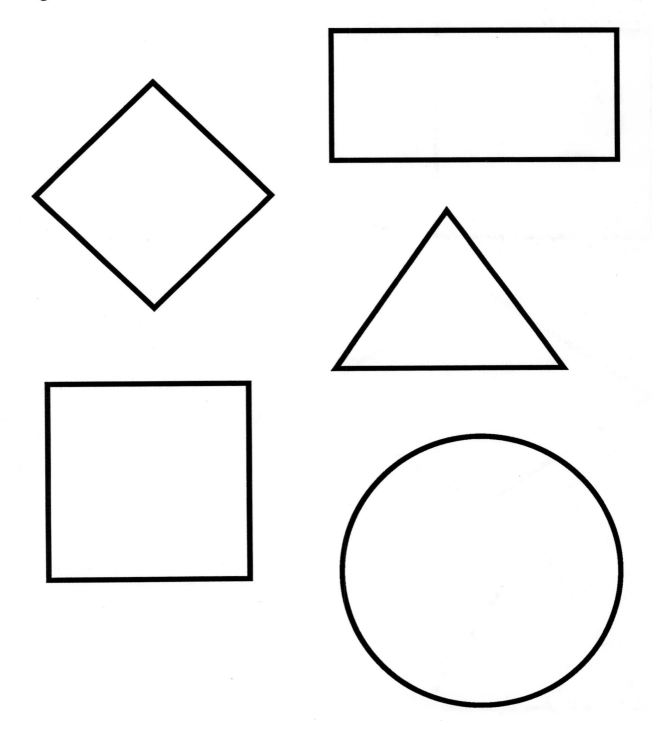

Playsheet
_____

 Toothpick Shapes
_____

Next to each shape, create the same shape with toothpicks and glue.
Then, on a blank sheet of paper, create your own Pretty Pick Picture!

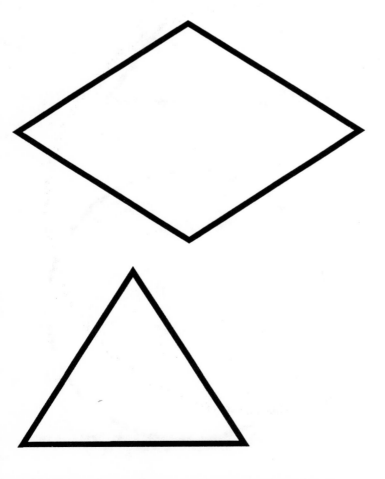

From *Hands-On Math*, published by Scott, Foresman and Company, Copyright © 1990 Janet Stone.

Playsheet

Shape Match

Look at the tracings below. For each tracing, find an object on the table that matches it. Glue the item to its tracing.

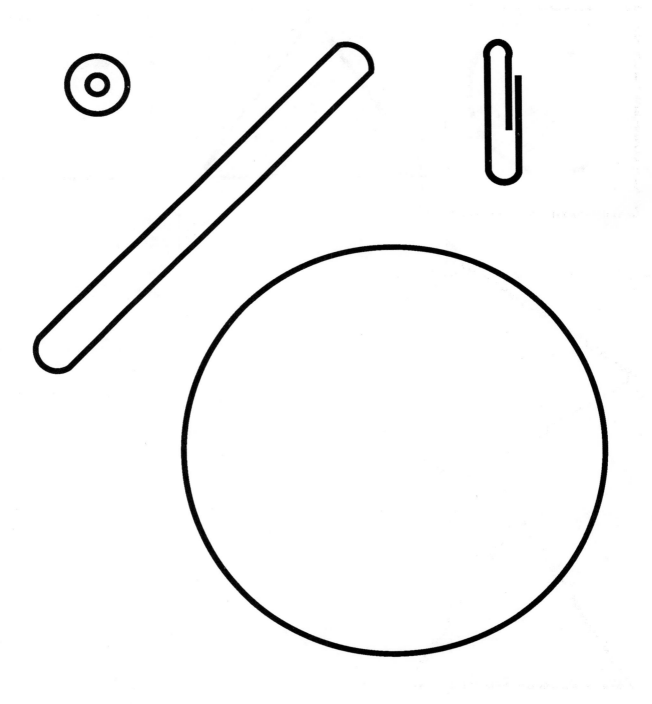

Playsheet

Sorting Shapes

Look at the shapes on the table. On this page, paste circles in the circle column, triangles in the triangle column, and squares in the square column.

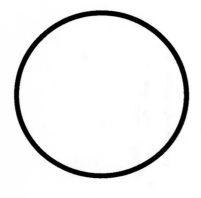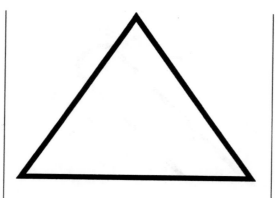

Playsheet _____

Cutters and Cookies

Cut out each cookie at the bottom of this paper. Paste each next to the cutter that could have made it!

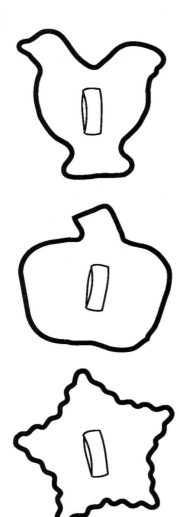

Playsheet

 Shapes on a Fold

Fold your paper on the dotted line. Press hard along the fold. Cut out with scissors along the solid lines. Open your cutouts and your paper . . . you may be surprised!

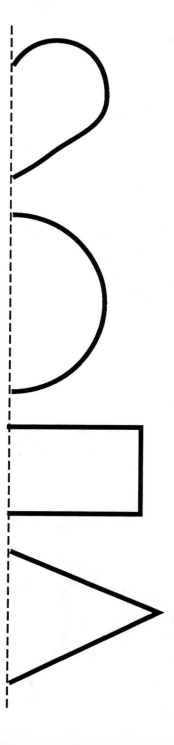

Playsheet

 Draw a Bigger One!

Look at the pictures below. Next to the lollipop, draw a bigger lollipop; next to the face, draw a bigger face; next to the cloud, draw a bigger cloud; and next to the fish, draw a bigger fish. Your picture may look very different from the one you see; just make sure to make it bigger!

Playsheet

Note Cards and Envelopes

Cut out each of the note cards at the bottom of this page. Paste each one over the envelope into which it would best fit (without being folded).

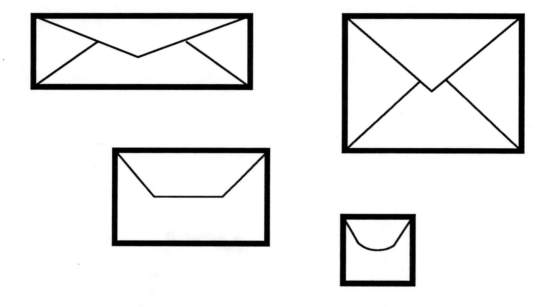

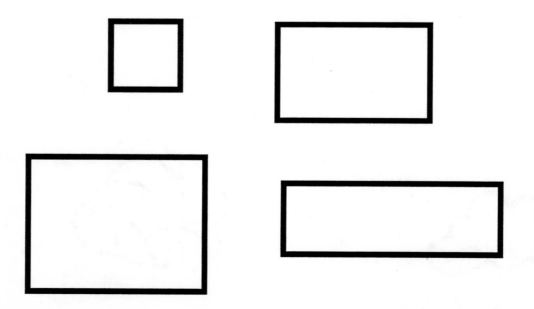

Playsheet

 Melting Candles

Using glue and red glitter, add a flame to each candle below. Next, draw a *shorter* candle beside each candle, to show how it will look after it burns for a while!

Playsheet

10 Doughnuts on Dishes

Pretend that the reinforcements on the table are tiny doughnuts. Stick *one* doughnut on each dish below. Try not to skip any dishes.

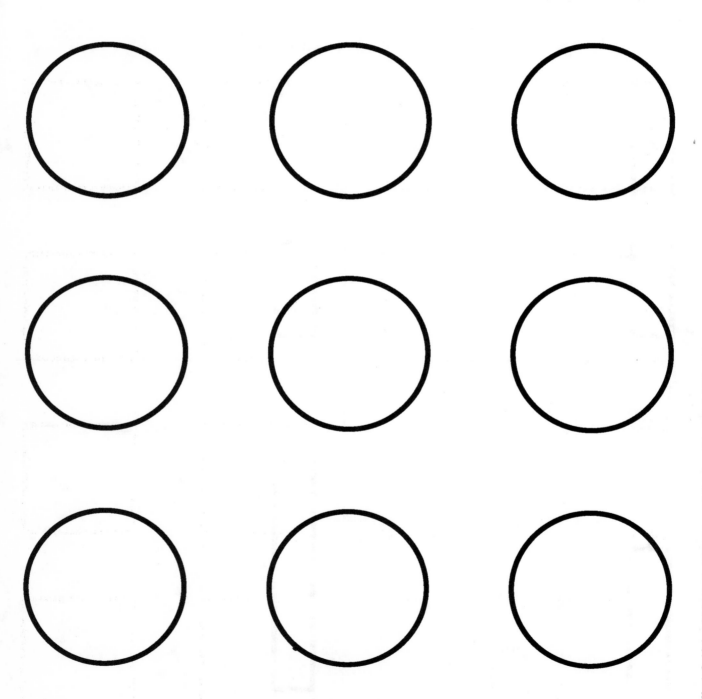

From *Hands-On Math*, published by Scott, Foresman and Company, Copyright © 1990 Janet Stone.

Playsheet

11 One-to-One Correspondence

Place one raisin in each square below. Try not to skip any squares. Now eat one raisin from each square below. If you do not skip any squares, all the squares will be empty again. Finally, stamp one time in each square and try not to skip any squares.

Playsheet

12 Go Togethers

Each item on the table (apple seed, kite string, ribbon, feather, button, and stamp) has something to do with a picture below. Glue each item next to the picture it belongs with.

Playsheet

13 Mitten Match

Cut out the mittens at the bottom of this paper. Glue each next to its mate! On the back, design your own pair of mittens.

Playsheet _____

14 Stick Fit

How many popsicle sticks will fit in the box below? Make a good guess (an estimate), then see how close you came by placing sticks in the box, side-by-side, with their sides touching. Place your first stick over the tracing of a stick, and your last stick over the other tracing of a stick; fit as many sticks in-between as you can. Glue them close together. Count them and circle the numeral that tells how many fit.

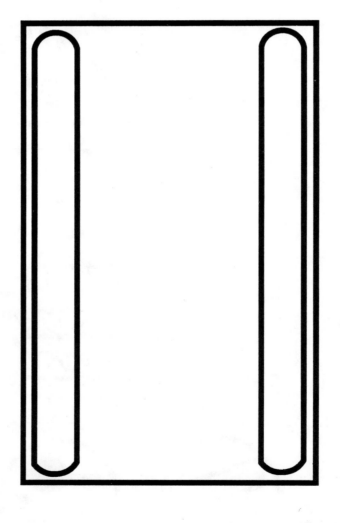

1   2   3   4   5   6   7   8

Playsheet

15 Bean Sets

For each set of shapes below, create an equal set of beans. After you have made your sets, cook and eat the beans, or plant them in soil, or glue them to your paper and take your sets home!

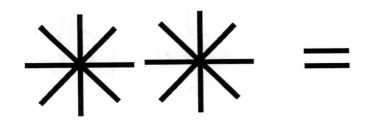

=

=

=

=

Playsheet

 The More, the Merrier!

Use a pencil or crayon to add more:

more hair!

more stripes!

more buttons!

more whiskers!

Playsheet

17 Follow-the-Dots

Draw lines from one dot to another to complete the picture below. Start at the dot next to the 1 and continue in numerical order. You will find a fun place to play! Draw yourself, peeking out!

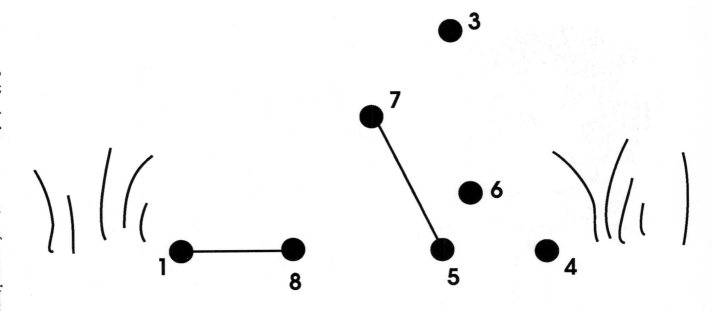

Playsheet

Fingerprint Bugs

In each box below, make as many fingerprint bugs as the numeral indicates. Use a pen to add antennae, eyes, and other features.

1	2
3	4
5	6
7	8

From *Hands-On Math*, published by Scott, Foresman and Company, Copyright © 1990 Janet Stone.

Playsheet

 Crazy, Mixed-Up Numerals

The numerals at the bottom of this page are mixed up; they are not in the right order. Cut them apart on the broken lines and paste them in the right order in the boxes at the top of the page. In the space that is left, try writing each numeral.

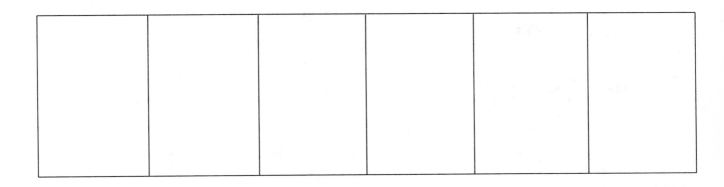

Playsheet

Fish on a String

Cut out the fish below. Use a hole punch to make a hole in each fish.
String them in numerical order,
and take home your catch!

Playsheet

21 Make a Face!

Use the yarn, glue, and face parts on the table to create an interesting face. Give it all the parts it needs.

Playsheet

22 Shape Puzzles

Teachers: Reproduce this page. Cut out any of the shapes you like and then cut them apart on the broken lines. Let the children find parts that go together and paste them together again on a sheet of construction paper.

Playsheet _____

23 Dot Addition

By pressing your eraser against a stamp pad, your eraser can become a stamp! Use it to print dots. Under each numeral in each addition problem below, print as many eraser dots as the numeral indicates. Then, for each problem, count all the dots to find the sum! Write the sum, or paste it, after the equals sign.

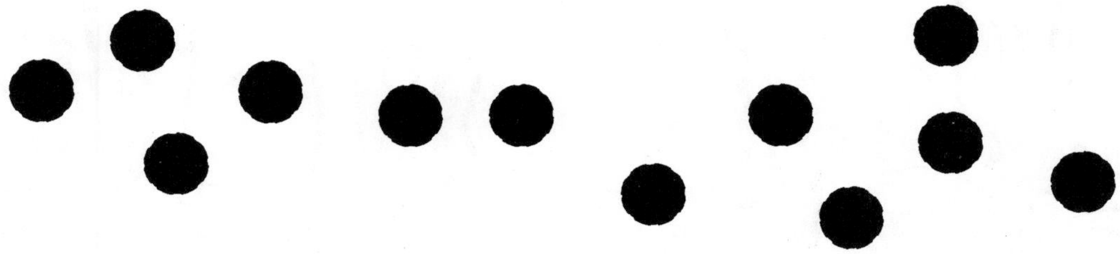

1 + 1 =

2 + 1 =

2 + 3 =

3 + 3 =

| 1 | 2 | 3 | 4 | 5 | 6 |

From *Hands-On Math*, published by Scott, Foresman and Company, Copyright © 1990 Janet Stone.

Playsheet

24 Disappearing Act

Be a magician! Use white shoe polish to make rabbits disappear and to solve each problem!

4 - 1 =

3 - 2 =

2 - 1 =

From *Hands-On Math*, published by Scott, Foresman and Company, Copyright © 1990 Janet Stone.

Playsheet

25 Ruler

Cut the rulers out and staple or tape them together to form a 12-inch ruler.

1	2	3	4	5	6	

7	8	9	10	11	12

Playsheet

26 Measured Lines

Lay your ruler under the numeral 2 below. Line up the start of your ruler with the line on the left of this paper. Using your pencil, make a 2-inch line; it will end under the numeral 2. Make a 3-inch line under the numeral 3, a 5-inch line under the 5, and a 6-inch line under the 6. Measure the line at the bottom of this paper and tell or write how long it is.

2

3

5

6

From *Hands-On Math*, published by Scott, Foresman and Company, Copyright © 1990 Janet Stone.